LICENSING TALES

Captivating Stories from Industry Legends

Greg Battersby

Kent Press

Westport, CT 06880

Kent Press
25 Poplar Plain Rd.
Westport, CT 06880
www.kentpress.com

This publication is designed to provide accurate and authoritative information regarding the subject matter covered. It is sold with the understanding that the publisher is not engaged in rendering legal, accounting, or other professional services. If legal or other professional assistance is required, the services of a competent professional person should be sought.

From a *Declaration of Principles* jointly adopted by a Committee of the American Bar Association and a Committee of Publishers and Associations.

First Edition
ISBN: 978-1-888206-16-6

Dedication

To Susan – my light, my NorthStar, my best friend. After 50 years of marriage, 3 start-up businesses, and now more than 55 books, I do not know how you withstood any of them. I do know, however, that I couldn't have done anything without you nor would I have ever wanted to. I could never imagine life without you.

Greg

Also, by Greg Battersby

Law of Merchandise & Character Licensing, Thomson Reuters

Licensing Law Handbook 1985, Thomson Reuters

NYIPLA Intellectual Property Law Annual, NYIPLA Press

The Toy & Game Inventor's Guide 1st and 2nd editions, Kent Press

The Essential Guide to Merchandising Forms, Kent Press

Multimedia & Technology Licensing Forms Annotated, Thomson Reuters

A Primer on Technology Licensing, Kent Press

An Insider's Guide to Royalty Rates 1st and 2nd editions, Kent Press

Licensing Law Handbook 1998, Thomson Reuters

Law of the Internet, Wolters Kluwer

Licensing Update (annually since 1999), Wolters Kluwer

Licensing Deskbook, Wolters Kluwer

Licensing Royalty Rates (annually since 2000), Wolters Kluwer

Drafting Internet Agreements: Forms and Analysis, Wolters Kluwer

License Agreement: Forms & Checklists, Wolters Kluwer

Trademark & Copyright Disputes: Litigation Forms and Analysis, Wolters Kluwer

Patent Disputes: Litigation Forms and Analysis, Wolters Kluwer

Basics of Licensing 1st and 2nd editions, Kent Press

Basics of Licensing: Licensee Edition, Kent Press

Basics of Licensing: International Edition, Kent Press

The Business of Licensing, Kent Press

Licensing Tales, Kent Press

Preface

After having worked in the licensing industry for almost half a century, I have been fortunate enough to have heard and even participated in some truly fascinating stories involving the industry. Lying awake one night, I thought someone should compile and memorialize some of the stories which have made the industry what it has become today. With that in mind, this book was born ... a collection of fascinating stories of the industry over the past half-century.

Fortunately, two things helped in the process. The first was not good for anyone other than, perhaps, me. The pandemic and the resulting lockdown that my fellow Northeasterners experienced gave me the time to work on the project without a lot of distractions.

The second was a much better thing and, no doubt, far more important. After reaching out to many industry leaders, I was honored to receive a raft of contributions from licensing colleagues who loved the idea and expressed a willingness to participate. Without those contributions, *Tales* would not have been possible.

I am always hesitant to name the myriad of contributors who helped for fear that I will leave an important person out. Nevertheless, in no particular order, the following contributed handsomely to this project: Dan Romanelli, Danny Simon, Dell Furano, Brian Hakan, Charles Riotto, Steve Herman, Allan Feldman, Mike Quackenbush, Charles Schnaid, Alan Dorfman, Carole Postal, Robert Strand, Louise Caron, Jerry Kapner, Jay Foreman, Mike Bowling, Jed Ferdinand, Ted Larkins, Francesca Ash, Arlene Scanlan, Nell Roney, Spencer Rosenheck, John McCann, Dan Lauer, Adam Berg, Michael Jonas, and Kalle Torma. If that sounds like a "Who's Who of Licensing," it's because it is. I appreciate all of those who took the time to share their experiences with me.

Also, I was fortunate enough to "borrow" some of the interviews that I had previously taken on behalf of the *Merchandising Reporter* and *The Licensing*

Journal with such lions of the industry like ~~Honest~~ Ed Justin, Jack Revoyr, Les Borden, Marty Blackman, Stan Jarocki, and Murray Altchuler.

Finally, a special call-out to my long-time editor, Michelle Houle, who helped immeasurably in compiling and editing the manuscript for which I am truly grateful.

Greg

Table of Contents

Dedication ii

Preface i

Table of Contents iii

I. Tales of Imaginative Agents 1

   ~~Honest~~ Ed Justin—The Early Years 1

   Highly Motivated & Highly Intelligent Les Borden 9

   Allan Feldman and the Genius of Bowling in a Snowstorm 10

   Murray Altchuler on LCA's Role in Licensing's Formative Years 12

      Setting Minimum Guarantees 15

II. Who Would Have Thought? 17

   Romanelli's Remembrances 17

      MICHAEL JORDAN, an Actor? 17

      SPACE JAM Sequel That Almost Didn't Happen 20

   Early UCLA Licensed Products Sold Better in Japan than California 20

      70% of Licensing Revenue Comes from Japan 22

III. Successful Properties from Left Field 25

   MICKEY MOUSE 25

   PEANUTS and SNOOPY 26

   CABBAGE PATCH KIDS 27

   TEENAGE MUTANT NINJA TURTLES 29

   How Licensees Discovered PAC-MAN 32

   A Yarn About Pom Poms on Tennis Socks 34

   Larkins on Licensing in Japan 35

   Carole Postal's Postings 38

IV. The Road Less Traveled 41

   IBM Licenses DOS Not CPM 41

   STAR WARS—If You Can't Buy it, Create Your Own 44

   ROCKY....Its Gotta Be Me 46

V. Stories from the Road & Licensing Expo 49

   Francesca Ash Reflects on Almost 40 Years of Licensing Expos 49

Blue Brothers Go to Vegas 50

Danny Simon's Ode to the Licensing Show.........................51

Louise Q. Caron's Recollections from LIMA Gala's Past 52

   Do You Know Who I Am?.. 52

   The Lion Sleeps Tonight 54

   Early LIMA Award Winners—Like a Door Prize?? 54

The Battle of Sixth Avenue..55

Steve Herman & Pizza to the Gala 55

VI. Unique Licensed Products.. 57

  Arlene Scanlan's Favorite Licensed Products 57

  Examples of Unique Licensed Products 59

VII. Auditing Trails 71

  Mike Quackenbush's Memories.......................................71

   Henry VIII Look-Alike Licensee 71

   Chinese Licensee's Multiple Set of Books 72

  Charles Schnaid's Remembrances 73

   Who Said You Can't Deduct Returns When Calculating Net Sales?........ 73

   The POOH Wars 74

   Double Dealing by a Licensee.................................. 74

   What Conflict of Interest? 75

VIII. The League of Mutual Destruction 77

  The BRATZ Wars 77

  WINNIE THE POOH....and Disney Too 79

IX. The Licensing Hall of Shame 83

  WWE Smacks Down Its Licensing Agents.........................83

  The Case of the Truncated Royalty Statements 85

X. Neat Inventions and Inventors..89

  TICKLE ME ELMO 89

  POUND PUPPIES 92

  TRIVIAL PURSUIT 95

  WATERBABIES® 97

XI. Celebrity Jeopardy 99

  Athletes & Beer Commercials 99

Mean Joe Green Commercial for Coca-Cola 100

Nell Roney on How SPUDS McKenzie Went from Fame to Shame......101

Arlene Scanlan on Rodney Dangerfield 103

Brian Hakan on Licensing with Kenny Rogers..........................104

   The Greatest Song.. 105

   The Gambler Slot Machine 106

   The Toy Shoppe 106

Jay Foreman on Dealing with Hollywood Stars 107

Celebrity Shorts...108

Dell Furano on how Marvel "Kiss Comic" Used Real Blood in Ink.......109

XII. Licensing Strands by Robert Strand 113

A Sign That It's Over...113

NBA Finals v. LIMA Awards Ceremony................................113

Micromanagement is Underrated.....................................114

Challenges to Licensing Interns 115

   Remember Michigan J. Frog?.................................. 116

   I Should Have Trademarked That.............................. 116

He's Trying to Waist Our Time 117

Ain't Too Proud to Beg 117

XIII. How I Got Started in Licensing................................... 119

Basic Fun's First License—SUPER SOAKER 119

Licensing at a Toy Company is Like Nowhere Else 120

Licensing Sure Beats Patent Prosecution 121

Kalle Torma Breaking in with Angry Birds 122

Louise Q. Caron – Colgate-Palmolive's Loss Was LCA's Gain 123

XIV. Cool Trademarks & Patents 125

Trademark Filings/Registrations......................................125

   Sports Themed.. 125

   Celebrities.. 125

   Colleges 126

   These Are Trademarks??? 126

Cool Patents 128

   Classic Toys 128

Iconic Products 129

Dolls & Figures.. 131

Puzzles and Board Games..................................... 132

Popular Characters 133

Iconic Sports Products 134

Star Wars Products 135

XV. Bits & Pieces 137

Adam Berg on Forming Friendships in Licensing................ 137

Sister Cathy Meets LJN President 138

Reflections by Steve Herman 138

Super Licensing Salesman 140

Michael Jonas—So You Want to Be a Millionaire?............. 142

Spencer Rosenheck—Full Chinese Escort 142

Best Deals Ever/Never Done by Jerry Kapner.................. 144

Greg Battersby's Best Excuse by a Licensee for Not Paying Royalties 144

Carole Francesca—Women in Licensing: We've Come a
Long Way Baby 145

XVI. The Lighter Side of Licensing 149

Garfield Comics 149

Peanuts Comics 149

Archie Comics Strips... 151

Other Comic Strips 152

Index.. 155

About the Author 170

I. Tales of Imaginative Agents

~~Honest~~ Ed Justin—The Early Years

The following is from an interview with Ed Justin in the Nov/Dec 1982 issue of *The Merchandising Reporter*. Surprisingly, while a lot has changed over these past 40 years, a lot remains the same.

MR: Can you tell us a little about your background? How long have you been in merchandising? How did you get into merchandising?

JUSTIN: I have been in merchandising since March of 1953. I was the Director of a summer camp for over-privileged girls and one of the parents of the girls was the head of NBC licensing. One day he asked me, "How would you like to be the General Manager of NBC licensing?" I said, "What's licensing?" He started confusing me for about ten minutes and finally, I said, "Forget it, what's it pay?" He told me and I said, "I'll learn."

They had an excellent licensing division headed up by Martin Stone who hired me. NBC had a terrifically over-staffed group doing the licensing for "HOWDY DOODY," even though it was not that big of a property. It just seemed like a big property in its time, but it did not make a lot of money. After Martin Stone left NBC, I became the head of licensing. I was very happy there except that they had promised me that my salary would be adjusted based upon performance. That promise was made by the Board of Directors and recorded in its minutes. In the first year, I increased their preceding net by 7 times. When I went to Mac Clifford, the Executive Vice President, initially to get a raise for the guys who worked for me who were largely responsible for the increase, he made me crawl for three or four visits and then finally gave them the money. When I went back to ask about an adjustment of my salary, given the 7 times increase, he said, "Your job isn't worth any more than what we pay you now." So, I called Columbia which had been offering me a job and went over there. I started at Columbia on April Fool's Day in 1956 and stayed until July 3, 1976. I formed Ancillary Enterprises on July 4, 1976, and I did a mailing piece, the heading of which was "Our Declaration of Independence."

MR: When did you first acquire your nickname "~~Honest~~ Ed Justin"?

JUSTIN: Since we are all peddling the same stuff in this business, you must have a gimmick if you want people to remember you. It's like show business. To keep people from throwing my mailing pieces away, I wanted to have some recognition. In the beginning, I used to have a lot of fun, political fun, so I signed the mailing pieces "Big Ed", which was a joke to those who knew me; and then somewhere along the line it got turned into "Honest Ed" and I've used that for twenty-five years

now. It has recognition value. People call on the telephone and ask for "Honest Ed with the Honest crossed out."

MR: *You've been in the business for over thirty years. In those years, what are the three hottest properties you have personally been involved with in merchandising?*

JUSTIN: Any three Hanna-Barbera properties. HUCKLEBERRY HOUND, YOGI BEAR, and FLINTSTONES were all incredible properties. FLINTSTONES is still a gigantic property. FLINTSTONES was originally intended to be an adult show. It was a straight take-off from the HONEYMOONERS. FRED FLINTSTONE was Jackie Gleason and BARNEY RUBBLE was Art Carney. The two women were the two sisters. I was having a very difficult time licensing the show because there was no appeal to kids. So, I called Bill Hanna, with whom I was close. I said, "Bill, I'm sending you a picture of a lovely little kid, I'd like to have a kid in the series named PEBBLES." Bill said it sounded like a good idea and so they made some drawings and I took the drawings to Ideal Toy who made three models. We sent the three models out to Hanna-Barbera and they chose the model they liked best and they animated that model into the series as PEBBLES.

 Several weeks later I had a big promotion planned with Ideal and, just before announcing the promotion, I was having lunch with the President. He said, "by the way, is PEBBLES a boy or a girl?" I said a boy and he said, "Hell, we could make much more money if PEBBLES was a girl. Dolls sell much better as girls." We went back to the office and, to give you an idea of how wonderful it was to work with Hanna-Barbera, they were the greatest, I called Joe Barbera and said, "Hey Joe, I made a terrible mistake, I'm here with the President of Ideal and he tells me we should have made PEBBLES a girl because we could make ten times as much money." Joe said, "Eddie, you want PEBBLES to be a girl?" I said "please" and he said, "okay". So, they changed a few lines of dialogue, and PEBBLES was a girl. A year later, I said we must have a boy to play with PEBBLES. I named the boy BAM BAM and described what he was to be. BAM BAM is the same model as PEBBLES but with a different set of hair and clothing. We did not have to make a new mold. No new drawings were needed.

MR: *What's an agent's role in merchandising?*

JUSTIN: It depends on the agent's relationship with the client. He can just be a flunky who runs around and tries to get licenses. Or, he can have a close enough relationship like I had with Hanna-Barbera that permitted me to create PEBBLES and BAM BAM. I have a similar relationship with people I work with in movies today. I try to read the treatment for a movie, not the screenplay, but the treatment, because a good agent can make suggestions early on which will cost the client absolutely nothing but which could be the basis for a licensing campaign. It doesn't always work, but the client has nothing to lose by letting me give my input. I just gave input on a movie to be called FUTURE GOLD. I must have outlined twenty-five suggestions on stuff that is touched on peripherally in the screenplay which, with modification, could have merchandising potential. For instance, the name of a gadget.

MR: How early do you get involved in your client's development of a property?

JUSTIN: As early as they will let me. With movie people, I frequently get them to rewrite scripts. I tell them the truth, which isn't a popular thing to do, but I can afford it. With BOOM-BOOM MANCINI I cannot do much. I can't spar with him.

MR: Are most studios now conscious or aware of the potential of merchandising?

JUSTIN: They're becoming conscious. They believe their hype. They are beginning to not only believe but **expect** big numbers. Now, if a guy does not produce a billion dollars in royalties, they think he's a bum. Most motion pictures are not licensable. At Columbia, I used to send out an annual memo saying let's revise our contracts with the performers and producers so that they have a fair share of the merchandising royalties so they will be cooperative. Most contracts are so unfair to the producers, i.e., they don't get anything, that they have no reason to go out of their way to help me. If an actor is getting screwed, why should he be cooperative? For example, in connection with the MONKEES, we did $3-4 million in royalties, but the four kids got practically nothing because they were sharing 5% of Columbia's net and in the motion picture business net is such a nebulous term. Those kids still hate me because they think I took their money. I never touched it. It went right to the company. Motion picture companies and everybody else have reached the point where they think you can spit on the sidewalk and if it falls into shape, you can license it. 99% of what is out in the field today shouldn't be licensed because it's hurting people. People are being  talked into creating toys and games and clothing items for properties that nobody is going to recognize. They are given a good sales talk and maybe lied to a little bit and they are talked into doing it. The motion picture companies are very guilty of this. Every motion picture they do they think should be the subject of a big licensing campaign.

MR: Why does a particular motion picture have merchandising potential?

JUSTIN: Luck. It must appeal to young people, under twenty. FAME happens to appeal to older people, people who go to dancing school, etc. but that is rare. Usually, the ages of your audience are from 5 to 18. They are the impulse buyer. I think my old HOWDY DOODY clients are now wearing clothing with DELAURENTIS and other idiot things they put on them though. It is the same foolishness. It's like wearing HOWDY DOODY to put DELAURENTIS on your shirt.

MR: *Does your FAME campaign differ from your previous campaigns with properties such as SATURDAY NIGHT FEVER?*

JUSTIN: Only to the extent that I am being much more demanding of the licensees. For example, I will not license an iron-on for FAME. That's unusual. I have such high regard for the property that I will not demean it or cheapen it by letting someone take an iron-on and stick it on just anything. I want it to be something I approve of. I didn't do that with SATURDAY NIGHT FEVER, but the life expectancy of SATURDAY NIGHT FEVER was so much less, I had to get the royalties while the property was hot.

MR: *Why does a property owner need an agent?*

JUSTIN: Property owners can't handle the licensing themselves. They will screw it up. Unless they hire somebody in-house. But nobody is a complete expert. No one can be in this business, whether he is an agent or an in-house employee. Let me tell you about a quick business story. A guy walked in here about the fifth or sixth week that SATURDAY NIGHT FEVER was in the theaters. By the way, I went to the first screening and I  hated it but I saw the reaction of the young girls in the audience and I told Fred Gershen and Robert Stigwood that I thought that the thing was going to make a fortune. Anyway, the guy walked in here several weeks after the movie was running and he told me who sent him and that he wanted a license for men's cut and sewn shirts for SATURDAY NIGHT FEVER. Now, my policy is don't do anything that will screw the clients. You can screw them once, but they will never come back. I still have clients I had with HOWDY DOODY in 1953. So I said to the guy, "Man, I could understand if you wanted a license for boys' or girls' but no sane man is going to go into a store and buy a SATURDAY NIGHT FEVER shirt and pay a premium." He said, "Listen, please, don't argue with me, don't tell me my business, how much do you want? I want a license." I was so embarrassed I gave him a license for practically nothing. I thought I was robbing the guy. I kept trying to talk him out of it and I said, "How are you going to use the logo, put it on the pocket?" He said, "No, it will be a sport shirt, no pocket." I said, "Geez, why are you going to give me the money, you'll have a hangtag on it which comes off and then that's it." He said, "No, where your shirt says, BROOKS BROTHERS, I'll use your SATURDAY NIGHT FEVER logo as a label." I thought to myself this guy is crazy. I took $2500 against a 6% royalty from him. About ten days or two weeks later, the guy comes back to the office with a grin a yard wide on his face and he says, "Hey Eddie, tell me the truth, you thought I was a dope didn't you?" I said, "Well if you put it that way, I sure didn't think you were smart." He said, "Well, I think you might like to see my opening order from J.C. Penny, I have it here, it's for $1,542,000." Opening order! J.C. Penney wound up doing television commercials, radio commercials, set-up special areas ***for a shirt that only had SATURDAY NIGHT FEVER in the collar as a label.*** Now, who can claim to be an expert? Believe me, I thought he was giving $2,500 away. I was ashamed to take the money.

MR: *Were you the one who was responsible for changing the original name of SATURDAY NIGHT FEVER?*

JUSTIN: Not really. I could claim credit, but there must be eleven people claiming credit. We said we couldn't license it with the original name, but that is not why they changed it. Everybody must have recognized that that original name, "The Tribal Rights of Saturday Night" was terrible. Can you imagine that on a shirt?

MR: *How do you go about promoting a property?*

JUSTIN: I have a victims list. I call them victims. I don't fool around. I send mailing pieces addressed "Dear Victim" to a long list which I have accumulated through all these years. The way I find out whether a property is going to have pizazz for merchandising is by the response I get from my people because they are all pros. If they respond to the property, then it's got a chance to make it. It may take time. For example, FAME did not get an instant response because it didn't make a big splash and it did not have a big star. It didn't have anybody you would recognize, but normally, you can tell by the response you get from your mailing pieces if something will make it in merchandising.

MR: *You list the National Ratings on one of your mailing pieces and I see LITTLE HOUSE ON THE PRAIRIE is on the National Ratings. Has that ever been licensed?*

JUSTIN: I don't think so. What are you going to license, sheep?

MR: *While you are trying to license the characters played by the two good looking girls on TOO CLOSE FOR COMFORT, what keeps those two girls from personally attempting to license themselves?*

JUSTIN: Nothing. So long as they don't refer to themselves as being in TOO CLOSE FOR COMFORT when they do their own personal licensing, there is no problem. One  of those girls did a poster, as an individual. The blonde girl. It was one of the sexiest posters you have ever seen. It dropped dead. She, as an individual, has no sales potential, her name doesn't mean anything. I have licensed a very sedate poster of the two girls with the words TOO CLOSE FOR COMFORT written across the poster and that's a pretty good seller. It's the show that's important. Of course, sometimes somebody breaks out of a show, as FARRAH FAWCETT did for a while, and becomes a hot property as an individual, but it's rare. I will give you a great example of what usually happens when they try to go it without the character association. One of the first properties I ever worked on was RIN TIN TIN. A great property. In it, we had a very handsome young guy. I think his name was JAMES BROWN. Good looking, talented with an excellent singing voice. I booked Madison Square Garden twice for the RIN TIN TIN show, filled the Garden for a week at a time, ten days at a time. JAMES BROWN, if he went out in his Lieutenant costume from the show with a big cavalry hat on, would pack the house. He refused to do that; however, he wanted to sing and get recognition as JAMES BROWN. He ended up singing in some dump for fifty bucks a night and I think there were two people in the audience. I went to hear him once. He was good, but it was sad, there was nobody there. When he went out connected with RIN TIN TIN, however, he was a giant, but when he went out on his own, he was a midget.

MR: What do you look for in a licensee?

JUSTIN: There are some I will not do business with because I know they steal too much. I expect them all to steal. In all the years of outside auditing, when I was at NBC and Columbia, we found only one mistake in our favor....and that one was funny. It involved Knickerbocker and they were NBC's first big licensee for Hanna-Barbera. We were responsible for making Knickerbocker a giant. They were a so-so company. Leo White, Ron's father, was a terrific guy, a great gambler and he liked what I showed him on Hanna-Barbera and he did a whole line—several HUCKLEBERRY HOUND's, several sizes of YOGI BEAR, PIXIE, etc. He did them all and he had a phenomenal year. The son of the President of Columbia Pictures was the head of business affairs, Burt Schneider, and he grew up in a hard world. He trusted nobody. He had a different sense of how to handle people than mine. Knickerbocker paid us $167,000 in royalties that first year. I can assure you that in 1956 or 58 that was an unheard-of amount of money. Nevertheless, Burt said to me, "what would happen if you didn't renew Knickerbocker's license?" I said, "I think they'd go bankrupt because the whole company is doing nothing else. I think Mrs. White takes home sewing. She sews dolls at night." Burt then said, "Well, suppose you tell them you won't renew the license unless they give us ten percent of the stock of their company?" I responded by calling the President and telling him, "I'll be right down with my resignation." The President asked, "What do you mean?" I replied, "I'm not in that type of business if Burt means what he says, I quit." Whereupon the President said, "Well you know that Burt's only kidding." I thought that they had forgotten about that, but Burt began to work me over. He said that because I did not want to extort 10% from Knickerbocker, I must be getting a kickback. So, every other day, Burt would ask "Do we ever audit Knickerbocker?" and I'd say, "Burt, they're our best client. They are so busy that they don't know what they are doing. They do nothing but make dolls for us. Why should I offend them, they could just as easily be overpaying as underpaying? Looking at their books won't tell us anything." Well, the more I said that the more convinced Burt was that I must be in cahoots with Leo White. So, I finally figured what the hell, I called Leo White and said, "I'm sorry, it's embarrassing to me, you're such a good licensee, but the company wants an audit." Leo said, "I don't care, send him today." Now they always send the dumbest guy in the accounting department, that's standard in all movie companies, because he's the guy that has nothing to do, he is hanging around doing nothing. So, the accountant goes to Knickerbocker's plant and he's there for three days. I don't know what he saw but he comes back and he's happy as a bluebird and he says, "Eddie, you should have seen the look on their faces when I told them they overpaid us $26,000.00." I said, "Congratulations, go tell it to Burt." So, he tells Burt and Burt comes up to me and says, "You're friendly with Leo White, aren't you? You can get him to settle that $26,000.00 for less, can't you?" I said, "Well, I'll try." So, I called Leo and said, "Leo, the jerk who did your books said you overpaid us $26,000. I said we'll give you a $15,000 credit for next year." To which he replied, "I'll take it."

That is not an extraordinary circumstance. Maybe with computers, you can keep better track. However, remember this, big companies make ten thousand items. Everything has got a number, even on the computer. Say I am number 996, do I know if they punch in 1096 for half of my property?

MR: Most merchandising properties find their genesis in motion pictures such as STAR WARS or E.T., is there room for the small property to be developed and hyped and become generated into a successful merchandising property? If so, what does it take?

JUSTIN: Well, first, it takes a certain amount of build-up in advance of the opening of the movie, otherwise nobody is going to be interested. Now, if you don't get into licensing in a movie before it opens, except for a STAR WARS or E.T., you're dead because movies do not last long enough for anybody to prepare anything. It takes time to make this stuff. It takes a preliminary build-up. It takes the reputation of the producer or the director or the names of the stars or the attraction of the story or the title or the property that is going to be made into a movie. If you're a little movie and you open quietly, forget it. It would have to be a super miracle.

MR: How about a non-movie property like STRAWBERRY SHORTCAKE? How did it become so successful?

JUSTIN: If you get a big greeting card company as a client, it's better than having a television series. Remember that they have access to more point-of-sale areas than anybody, except for breakfast cereal companies. You get Hallmark or you get American Greetings and they give you a fair shake, you're in every nook and cranny in the country. Your property almost automatically becomes important. I will tell you that Hallmark, in my opinion, was tremendously responsible for the success of PEANUTS. I had a t-shirt licensee who was then the biggest in the business. He called me one day, many, many years ago, and asked, "Do you know anything about what happened to PEANUTS? We have had the license for years and every year we have sold maybe a thousand dozen of them. Suddenly we're selling a thousand of them every day." The answer was that Hallmark had taken PEANUTS and had  done a beautiful job of creating a line of PEANUTS cards and, suddenly, PEANUTS was out in front of everybody's face in every little store in the country. Tens of thousands of locations. As a result, suddenly it was a major licensing property. American Greetings became sensible with STRAWBERRY SHORTCAKE, they had been promoting someone else's property for years. So why not promote their own property?

MR: How about something like a designer label?

JUSTIN: That's a whole different ball game. That is for the grown-ups who used *to* be HOWDY DOODY fans. It's just as dopey. The designers usually don't see the products on which their name appears. I knew the guy who used to do CARDIN men's clothing. He had a contract with CARDIN but no doubt that CARDIN ever saw his suits...unless he got one for nothing.

MR: What is the lowest royalty you have ever seen?

JUSTIN: On breakfast cereal, I did PEBBLES breakfast cereal, I think we got a fraction of a penny. You're talking millions and millions of sales, so it's worth it.

MR: You talked about sending auditors out to ensure that the royalty obligations are met.

JUSTIN: Quite frankly, it is a waste of time. I have a simple philosophy. I do not mind being cheated a little bit. If you are doing well enough and a guy wants to take a little advantage of you, it's not the end of the world. But if I feel a guy is overdoing it, I'll never do business with him again.

MR: What do you do when the client is complaining about an infringer, but you decide it is not worth it to sue?

JUSTIN: I talk the infringer into stopping. I'm good at that. I have had very good luck with discouraging infringers just by conversation, threatening letters, etc. I very, very rarely have been involved in litigation and I have had very little trouble with clients where infringement is not making a dent in our business. J.C. Penney, Sears, Montgomery Ward, Kmart will not buy from infringers. They will only buy from licensees. If infringers sell some store on Third Avenue in New York (i.e., some "back alley" shops), what's the difference?

MR: What was the biggest product for somebody like Hanna-Barbera and the FLINTSTONES property? What type of product?

JUSTIN: FLINTSTONES vitamins and YOGI BEAR'S JELLYSTONE PARK Campgrounds, which are still in existence. It's very big money. Those are properties that are here to stay forever.

MR: Who came up with the idea of the 'JELLYSTONE PARK Campgrounds?

JUSTIN: I did. I licensed every one of them, drew up contracts, I didn't know what I was doing, but I did it.

MR: What did you tell the Campground owners? Why should he pay you a percentage of his take? What were you giving in return?

JUSTIN: I saw the use of JELLYSTONE for camps as being a very good idea to attract

families with kids. We let the guy have an employee in a YOGI BEAR costume running around the park, posing for pictures and shaking hands with the kids and we let HUCKLEBERRY HOUND run around as well.

MR: Have you been grossly disappointed in any property that you believed in, i.e., a property that just never made it?

JUSTIN: Yes. Way back at NBC, our licensing division produced a show called JOHNNY JUPITER and I'll tell you it was created by some of the most imaginative people I've ever known in my whole life and it had every conceivable gimmick in it. It was a wonderful show and it even had a ready-made slogan, "Buy Jupiter". JOHNNY JUPITER was a puppet who came down to visit Earth on an electronic beam from Mars or someplace to a television station. It was a fabulous show. The guy who was then still the President of NBC, who hired me, was great but made a classic error. He developed the show expecting to lose say $1,000.00 or $1,500.00 per episode on production on the theory that we were nevertheless going to make millions on the licensing. He did not make one cent on licensing. Not a penny.

Highly Motivated & Highly Intelligent Les Borden

Excerpts from an interview with Columbia Picture's then Licensing Director, Lester Borden, in the *Merchandising Reporter* in 1983:

MR: Please tell us a little bit about yourself, your background, and how you came to Columbia Pictures Merchandising.

BORDEN: I am highly intelligent and highly motivated. Seriously, I have a BA, an MA, and an MBA. I'm starting my seventh year with Columbia this November. Previously, I had worked for NBC and a children's wear company. I came to Columbia through

a headhunter. I was hired as the Marketing Director. Four years ago, the guy who was Vice President left and I became Vice President. I did not know much about merchandising *per se* when I came to Columbia, except that I had always liked SNOOPY. I used to marvel at SNOOPY. I quickly found that merchandising is a combination of my previous work at NBC and the children's wear company. Merchandising is a very creative and very stimulating endeavor. One of the things I like about merchandising is that you're called upon to be creative and come up with properties that please people.

MR: You say you are a member of the Licensing Industry Association. Is that an active Association? Does the Association publish a directory?

BORDEN: I guess it is an active Association. They have 56 members or something like that. They publish a directory but there are a lot of people there that I have never heard of. It is a business that everyone is into. You have the guys representing the clothing lines, guys representing artwork, etc., and everybody has a property to license.

I get people calling me up about ridiculous properties. I expect the next call I will get will be from someone who has a property named POLLYANNA THE PIG, and they will want me to represent it. They will say it can be great for merchandising. I'll ask what it does? The answer will be it sweats, more than that, it makes *pink sweat.* What do I do? Take on the property and license pink sweat?

Allan Feldman and the Genius of Bowling in a Snowstorm

Have you ever wondered where some of the greatest ideas for brand extension licensing came from? Here is the story about one of the most interesting sources of some of the world's most successful and iconic brand licensing programs.

It was that time of the year again … January. The entire staff at LMCA would come together each year for a dedicated 2-3 day-long meeting to discuss the pros and cons of the past year in brand extension licensing, what we learned, and how we could do a better job going forward.

This year, one member of the team thought it would be good to start the meeting with an exercise intended to build the team spirit. "Let's go bowling together!" I think he had taken a psychology course in college and was adamant about this being a good way to get the ball rolling. So, we did!

We reserved a lane at Bowlmore Lanes, Greenwich Village, NYC. A great place, a lot of history, and they had all the right shoe sizes available. We scheduled to meet there at 9:00 am sharp. It was the first week of January, the 3rd or 4th I believe.

Little did we know that our kick-off date was going to bring one of the worst snowstorms in New York City history. By 9:00 am, 14-15" of snow had already fallen and the blizzard was in full tilt. Regardless, everybody showed up! We had the place to ourselves. It was the bowling alley owner/manager, maybe one employee … and the 14 of us.

We went from 9:00 to noon in this otherwise empty bowling alley and bowled what felt like an endless number of games. Our spiritual leader for this, Mr. Psychology, had us doing all kinds of teammate changes and run-offs and playoffs, etc. I don't remember much impact on team spirit/unity... but what was clear is that he liked bowling. He beat the pants off everybody!

Tired of bowling and hungry, it was time for lunch. It was still blizzarding outside, but we lucked out ... just down the street was a pub restaurant. We could make out through the snow that their lights were on and the place was open. They fit together 4 or 5 tables for us. After a few appetizers and some drinks, we ordered and started feeling OK.

MENSA BRAINSTORMING

We decided we were going to just stay at the pub after having lunch and begin our meeting ... how could we do better in the coming year. It was mid-lunch, and everybody was talking ... there were 6 or 7 different conversations taking place at the table. There was a din of noise ... but suddenly, some words were heard ... "MENSA BRAINSTORMING." All conversations stopped ... there was absolute silence, you could hear a pin drop. WHAT?? It was like striking gold. I think a hamburger fell out of someone's mouth onto the table or floor.

Serious brainstorming was always a hallmark of LMCA. From day #1 of the firm, we took great strides to identify unique and powerful brand extensions for our clients that could generate strong results. Caps, t-shirts, and the usual merchandise of most licensing programs of the time were not of interest ... we wanted to reach way beyond that and did so by bringing together diverse groups of creative people to identify high fit/high potential extension possibilities. Augmenting that group with MENSA geniuses would catapult/supercharge the process and bring it to a whole new level.

You see, the MENSA organization was one of our licensing clients. We had worked with them for about a year then and enjoyed it. They were brilliant (with an IQ in the top 2% of human intelligence), they were enthusiastic, and they had a great sense of humor. Their minds were wondrous ... they could get to places in the speed of a bullet that others might never reach. And there were nearly 100,000 of them spread throughout the world. Harnessing that power for LMCA brainstorming ... WOW!

Even to this day, we were never sure who among the team first uttered those words. I think it was Tim, one of our licensee solicitation managers ... a Penn State football star and graduate of the Army's famous 101st Airborne unit. He jumped out of planes with a parachute. Whatever, it was a great day!!

MENSA Process Becomes Prodigy Works

Shortly after that snowy team meeting, LMCA entered a joint venture with the MENSA organization and created the MENSA Process. The unit has evolved and expanded since its beginning in 1991 to become PRODIGYWORKS, one of the most sought-after innovation resources for the licensing industry and well beyond. Today, in addition to thousands and thousands of MENSA geniuses from all over the globe, this exceptionally diverse brain trust includes thousands of super creative thinkers, including artists, musicians, writers, poets, choreographers, comedians, Hollywood actors and more.

Now, in addition to brainstorming for brand licensing, PRODIGYWORKS capabilities extend into product innovation, new product development, process innovation, naming, and future work to help companies better understand emerging trends, shifts in consumer preference, and competitive threats – before they occur. PRODIGYWORKS has brought diverse and rapid high-IQ outside thinking to dozens of the world's leading companies and best-loved brands. Successes range from iconic white-space innovation for brands like HP, ARM & HAMMER, SNUGGLE, and KRAFT FOODS, to product innovation for companies like BAZOOKA CANDIES, SIMMONS BEDDING, OREO cookies, and HEINEKEN beer, to process innovation for companies as diverse as PFIZER and CHICK-FIL-A, and future for companies such as GEORGIA PACIFIC, the TOY ASSOCIATION, and CHASE FINANCIAL.

MENSA is an unbelievably diverse and incredibly eclectic group of fascinating, passionate problem solvers, and PRODIGYWORKS takes unique combinations of these creative geniuses and unleashes them on companies' toughest challenges. The LMCA-PRODIGYWORKS journey has been an interesting one, to say the least, and we've only just begun to explore the extent of the capabilities of this incredibly rich global resource. Stay tuned for more.

Murray Altchuler on LCA's Role in Licensing's Formative Years

The following is an excerpt from an interview with Murray Altchuler in the Nov/Dec 1983 issue of *The Merchandising Reporter* before he left LCA to form LIA and then LIMA.

MR: When was LCA (Licensing Corp. of America) started and by whom?

Altchuler: LCA was started in the early 1960s by two individuals, Jay Emmett and Allan Stone. Neither of them is still affiliated with the company.

MR: When did LCA become part of Warner Bros.?

Altchuler: In the late 1960s. Up through 1968, the major properties that projected LCA to its growth pattern, to where it is today, were BATMAN, which went on television in 1966, and the JAMES BOND movies. They were two very important properties at that time and were very profitable and contributed to the positive position of the company. BATMAN was the property of a company known as National Periodical Publications, the publisher of the comic book. Today that same company is known as DC Comics. National Periodical Publications bought LCA  around 1968. Then there was a progression of mergers whereby National Periodical Publications was acquired by the company that is known as Warner Communications Inc. LCA, which is a subsidiary of National Periodical Publications, was part of the purchase. Today, we are a wholly owned subsidiary of Warner Communications.

MR: What is your current role at LCA?

Altchuler: I am presently a Vice President. I have been given a new assignment, to exploit a category that we think we have not done as good a job as we've done in other areas. I am on a new project for the company in the area of stationery, gifts, novelties, and accessories. We think we have an opportunity there that will give us important growth.

MR: Does LCA get involved in either the sports or the corporate logo licensing areas?

Altchuler: Yes. LCA has a mandate from management to seek out whatever properties we feel have merchandising or licensing potential. We are heavily involved in sports licensing. We are the licensing agent for MAJOR LEAGUE BASEBALL, for the names, graphics, logos of all 26 clubs. We are also the licensing agent for the NATIONAL HOCKEY LEAGUE, for the 21 NHL clubs. Also, we are the licensing agent for two sports associations, the NATIONAL HOCKEY LEAGUE PLAYERS ASSOCIATION and NATIONAL FOOTBALL PLAYERS ASSOCIATION. So, I suspect in terms of properties, we are as involved as anyone in the world in sports. If you want to put another sports orientation next to it, we are also the licensing agent for DOROTHY HAMILL, the past Olympic Gold Medal winner of Figure Skating. That's our sports involvement.

MR: And corporate logo licensing?

Altchuler: LCA is not involved in corporate logo merchandising and licensing at this time.

MR: Could you give us an example of a company involved in corporate logo licensing?

Altchuler: COTTON INCORPORATED is one example. They merchandise the COTTON logo. HERSHEY, ANHEUSER BUSH, COCA-COLA, and STETSON are others. These people have corporate logos which the public is very aware of. They have spent a lot of money creating public awareness of their logos. Because of that awareness, their corporate logos have merchandising potential.

MR: LCA appears to go further than most agencies, that is most agencies typically have only one person or maybe two who handle each property.

Altchuler: Yes. For example, we have seven people that will sell baseball. If the product area is toys and games, it will be handled by individual A; if it's gifts, stationery, novelties, accessories, it will go to person B; if it's infants and children's apparel, it will go to person C; if it's male sports apparel, it will go to person D. There is a logic behind our system, it is not an arbitrary breakdown. When you search out and analyze manufacturers, you do so by their product lines and what their capabilities are, by the types of accounts they sell, by the types of products they make. You consider if their product line is sold upstairs or downstairs in stores, is it

mass merchandise, do they distribute through their own sales force or jobbers or reps. If you have a company that makes a long line of boy's jackets and/or shirts, for example, they may be interested in baseball properties we represent, and the hockey properties and the SUPERMAN property. If someone represented baseball at LCA and someone else represented hockey and a third person represented SUPERMAN, we would have three people soliciting that same manufacturer. I don't have to tell you that after the third call, he would get a little annoyed. So, instead, with our system, in one visit, we present him with an inventory of our properties and bring along an expert in the child field and say, "Let's discuss hockey" or "Let's discuss baseball" or "Let's discuss SUPERMAN". Theoretically, we've done enough homework to know that his size line is not good for baseball, because he only makes jackets for infants and toddlers and maybe that's too young, but then we'll know that his product line is good for Warner Brothers because BUGS BUNNY is skewed strongly to pre-school ages. Conversely, we may conclude his product line is not good for Warner Brothers because he is making teen jackets, and we feel the Warner Brothers properties are better targeted to the young element. So, we'll suggest sports properties.

MR: How did LCA set its financial parameters for a license?

Altchuler: We've learned over the years that we can have a licensee that could sell $1 million worth of goods, make us a reasonably substantial royalty, and yet 80% of that business or 100% could be with one major account. Now, we've made some good money, but are we performing our function for ourselves and our client? Are we meeting a mandate of distribution? We are not. The product is not in the marketplace. If he did $1 million, maybe there's a potential for $20 million. So, we ask what type of accounts he is selling to and a percentage of their volume and we break it down into specific categories: national chains, regional chains, department stores, buying offices, discount stores, drug stores, food stores, convenience stores, catalog, toy stores and, in case we miss anything, we say "others". At that stage, we ask him to do a little

14

homework. Too often, a prospective licensee figures the license will be the panacea for instant success, i.e., all he must do is place a label on a product and it will sell. We have had on occasion over the years where companies that are financially in trouble think that a license is going to pull them out of a financial dilemma. So, we ask him if he had the license, what are his sales projections? What is he going to do in the first year and in the second?

Setting Minimum Guarantees

Here is where we are probably a lot different than, I suspect, most of the trade. To my knowledge, every licensor works on a royalty, credited against a guarantee. Historically, my experience has been that the guarantee asked for by most licensors is pulled out of the air, based on experience, what he thinks the traffic will bear, etc. We don't do that. If you fill out our form as a prospective licensee, you state, for example, that in year one you expect to sell $500,000 worth of merchandise, and in year two you expect to sell $600,000 worth of merchandise. When this comes back to me, I'll look at it, and if I'm working, as an example, with a 7% royalty of wholesale, I don't have to be a genius to say 7% of $500,000 is $35,000 in royalties in year one. I will call him up and if we think $35,000 is not worth the product category, I will say so at that point and that becomes the subject of additional discussion. If we feel $35,000 is enough, I will say to him, "I told you beforehand that our royalty is 7% so that, using your $500,000 projection which would result in royalties of $35,000 in the first year, we want a $20,000 or $25,000 guarantee. At that point, if he says to me: "$20,000 or $25,000, I can't pay, it's too large a guarantee", we are almost at the end of the conversation because I can then only think that he just put the number $500,000 down without any basis or thinking. That is one of the warning flags we get from using our form. Rather than arbitrarily saying we want a $5,000 or $50,000 guarantee, we let the prospective licensee determine his own destiny. He decides what the guarantee he is willing to give us and we decide whether it is acceptable for the product category.

II. Who Would Have Thought?

Romanelli's Remembrances

MICHAEL JORDAN, an Actor?

MICHAEL JORDAN, the basketball legend, a successful actor? Who would have thought? Well, Dan Romanelli, Warner Bros. then head of consumer products did, and the results proved him correct. Particularly, an actor who had to switch between sweaty practice shorts and in-depth conversation with a cartoon character. To make the concept even more implausible, it all happened when JORDAN was in-between careers, having retired from basketball to pursue a career in baseball.

The merger of Jordan and Romanelli was the merger of two heavyweights in their respective fields. Romanelli had founded and built Warner Bros Consumer Products into a World-Class Organization with many of the best licensing executives in the industry. Among other things, he launched the Warner Bros Studio Stores and spearheaded some of the most heralded licensing campaigns of all time, including LOONEY TUNES, SPACE JAM, BATMAN, SUPERMAN, SCOOBY DOO and HARRY POTTER. In the 23 years he was at Warner Bros., his group generated over $100 billion at retail, worldwide. He is, quite deservedly, a member of LIMA's Licensing Hall of Fame.

This all led to the movie SPACE JAM, which opened in 2000 featuring MICHAEL JORDAN and the LOONEY TUNES characters. The movie, which was part animation and part live-action, involved a basketball game against cartoon aliens called the Monstars. Other professional basketball players, including PATRICK EWING, MUGGSY BOGUES, and CHARLES BARKLEY, made cameo appearances.

While the movie was universally panned by the critics (although Roger Ebert called it "a happy marriage of good ideas — three films for the price of one"), fortunately, the public disagreed. It earned more than $90 million domestically at the box office and $230 million worldwide. From a merchandising point of view, it was a blockbuster, yielding more than a billion dollars in retail sales. That is why Romanelli was so supportive of the project. Moreover, it is still the all-time, highest-grossing basketball movie.

How did the idea of pairing a basketball superstar with cartoon characters originate? It grew out of a Nike "HARE JORDAN" ad campaign that had been developed for airing during the SUPER BOWL. Jim Riswold, the creative director at Wieden+Kennedy, conceived the idea after working on commercials that paired

JORDAN with Spike Lee playing the character, MARS BLACKMON. Riswold said that Nike "wanted to do something different for the SUPER BOWL, so I couldn't think of a greater star than BUGS BUNNY to put him with" since the character was one of his childhood favorites.

Riswold thought that the pairing was a good match, explaining, "to be honest, a lot of athletes aren't good actors because they have better things to do than be good athletes. You put someone up with them to do the talking. MARS BLACKMON and BUGS BUNNY can both talk the balls off a statue."

Warner Bros. first had to decide which version of BUGS BUNNY to use—the present-day version or the one from the 1940s where he used to blow things up with dynamite. They concluded that the older version would not be acceptable to modern tastes.

The final product, HARE JORDAN, in which BUGS BUNNY and MICHAEL JORDAN joined forces to defeat the bad guys on the court, cost about a million dollars to produce. It proved to be money well spent because it was the most talked-about advertisement from the 1992 SUPER BOWL. BUGS BUNNY perhaps best summed it up when he said at the end of the ad, "This could be the beginning of a beautiful friendship." Another HARE JORDAN commercial would follow.

Perhaps an ad—even a popular one—but a JORDAN movie? Could he act???? JORDAN had turned down dozens of movie roles over the years, frequently being told that he could not act. What made this opportunity special, however, is that Warner Bros. was not intending to ask him to act—they simply wanted him to play himself.

It wasn't, however, an instant sell. Dan Romanelli got a call from JORDAN's agent who told him that Warner Bros. had turned down the opportunity to do the movie concept. Romanelli was flabbergasted, stating, "How can you not do something with MICHAEL JORDAN?" Above all else, Romanelli saw enormous licensing potential with plush toys and action figures. "I've been wrong about other things, but I felt like with Michael, you just can't go wrong. He's gold," Romanelli said.

Romanelli's excitement was not, however, universally shared by Warner Bros. management. They didn't want to "mess around" with BUGS BUNNY unless there was a good reason to do so. Romanelli won out, however, as management came to recognize that the potential dynamics between MICHAEL JORDAN and BUGS BUNNY could be fantastic.

Warner Bros. then assembled a strong team, including Joe Pytka, who had directed the HARE JORDAN ads, and Ivan Reitman, as the producer. Together, they conceived the idea of having JORDAN help the LOONEY TUNES characters in a basketball game against the MONSTARS.

Another problem surfaced. Just when things were starting to come together, JORDAN decided to retire from basketball to pursue a baseball career. Fortunately, or unfortunately depending upon how one looked at it, his baseball career did not turn out the way he had hoped. That brought Michael back into training for a basketball comeback. To support the return, Warner Bros. built a gym on the set for a not so insignificant amount. The PR and goodwill value of the investment overcame any cost, because it made him the star of the lot, drawing actors, executives, and staff for pickup games and workouts. He also brought along fellow pro and college players for competition.

Bill Murray joined the cast because of Reitman's prior experience with him. Murray would have one of the classic lines in the movie when he asked JORDAN why there wasn't any room in the NBA for a guy like him, adding, "It's 'cause I'm white, isn't it?" JORDAN responded, saying "No. Larry's [Bird] white." Murray retorted, saying, "Larry's not white. Larry's clear."

SPACE JAM was one of the first movies that adopted the concept of product placement, i.e., where consumer product companies pay a sponsorship fee to have their product appear in the movie. Among the sponsored products were GATORADE and WHEATIES. The movie score produced such megahits as R. Kelly's "I Believe I Can Fly," which won a Grammy, and Seal's "Fly Like an Eagle."

Another first for SPACE JAM was the use of Internet marketing to promote it which was in its infancy in 1995. Warner Bros. set up a website to describe how the motion picture was made. Finally, it used cutting edge computer animation to replace the animation done by hand in earlier movies.

Romanelli was quite proud of his role in convincing Warner Bros. to pursue the project. He described his efforts in doing so as one of his "proudest moments" at Warner Bros. His enthusiasm and vision were certainly borne out in the marketplace as more than $1 billion in licensed SPACE JAM merchandise was sold. "I remember one of the international executives said he thought we were very lucky with that," Romanelli recalled. "Luck had nothing to do with it. It all had to do with MICHAEL JORDAN and the LOONEY TUNES characters, and a really fun, sweet story that resonated with fans all around the world."

Romanelli's enthusiasm wasn't necessarily shared by director Riswold, who had come up with the original partnership of JORDAN and BUGS BUNNY. He said SPACE JAM was "a marketing idea first, and a movie, maybe ninth…. [but] that's okay. It made a lot of people smile, and we all know the world could use more smiling."

SPACE JAM Sequel That Almost Didn't Happen

While SPACE JAM was a hit in 1996, it took many stops and starts and decades before it yielded a sequel to become a Hollywood "franchise." Finally, 25 years after the SPACE JAM release, SPACE JAM 2 became a reality with LEBRON JAMES, RYAN COOGLER, and a lot of nostalgia and is scheduled for release in 2021.

The original plan was to have a traditional sequel to SPACE JAM. Warner Bros. had the original director, Joe Pytka, onboard and believed that MICHAEL JORDAN was ready to sign on as well. The plot would have been JORDAN and the LOONEY TUNES gang square off against a villain called Berserk-O played by Mel Brooks. When JORDAN refused, Warner Bros. considered other proposals, including:

- **Race Jam**, which would have pitted BUGS BUNNY against the highly popular race car driver, JEFF GORDON. Unfortunately, that movie never materialized.
- **Spy Jam** with JACKIE CHAN paired with BUGS BUNNY in a spy theme sequel. While that movie never materialized, the concept led to an unrelated movie called LOONEY TUNES: BACK IN ACTION in which JEFF GORDON from Race Jam fame had a cameo appearance.
- **Skate Jam** would have combined the LOONEY TUNES characters with skateboarder, TONY HAWK. Unfortunately, the lack of success of the Warner Bros. BACK IN ACTION movie was too much for management to overcome.
- **SPACE JAM: A New Legacy.** Four times is a charm. The above-described sequel to SPACE JAM was filmed in 2019 and scheduled for release in 2021. In addition to LEBRON JAMES and BUGS BUNNY,

  the movie will include a cast of the basketball elite, including ANTHONY DAVIS, DAMIAN LILLARD, KLAY THOMPSON, CHRIS PAUL, and WNBA Stars NNEKA OGWUMIKE and DIANA TAURASI Malcolm D. Lee directed it and it featured popular actor DON CHEADLE. Will it be a licensing powerhouse like its predecessor? Don't bet against it.

Early UCLA Licensed Products Sold Better in Japan than California

The following is an excerpt from an interview with Jack Revoyr, the former licensing director at UCLA which ran in the *Merchandising Reporter* in 1985:

MR: When did UCLA first get active in licensing?

Revoyr: It was about 1973. Before that time, I don't think the manufacturers were aware of the potential of collegiate marks in the general market and it was from the manufacturers that the real impetus for licensing came.

The history of UCLA is an interesting one. When it was founded in 1919, a group of students went to the then Chancellor and told him they wanted some services, you know, a store, a food service, sports and all the other services which are now taken for granted by students. That Chancellor said something which I think was brilliant. He said a University's function was to educate them. If they wanted all the other services, they were going to have to provide them for themselves. As a result, Associated Students (ASUCLA) was formed with the Chancellor's blessing to handle all these services for the students. Until about 20 years ago, dormitories, parking, and even the Athletic Department were part of ASUCLA and John Wooden was one of its employees. It was only after those services got so big that they were spun off. But ASUCLA still operates the campus store and food services as well as the vending machines on campus. It has a professional executive director, but it is directed by a board that is controlled by student members with representatives from the administration. The Licensing Department is part of ASUCLA.

MR: How long has UCLA been selling emblematic merchandise?

Revoyr: The student store began selling emblematic merchandise back in the 1930s and has continued to do so. We do not have a situation here where there is a lot of off-campus competition directly across the street. There were one or two stores that did sell some emblematic merchandise with our approval, or at least our acknowledgment, for some time. Even in the early days, however, our records show that the store directors did make a conscious effort to stop the unauthorized sale of UCLA merchandise. While it was an informal program, they continually sent out letters saying, "Hey, you can't do that."

Initially, the emblematic merchandise was scattered throughout the store. In 1973, however, a separate department or division of the store was created called "Bear Wear" and all the emblematic merchandise from the various departments was pulled together. Last year, the Bear Wear department sold close to $4 million worth of products. Total sales of the store last year were about $24 million.

In the early 1970s, the general counsel of the Regents of the University of California advised the Regents that the authority to authorize the commercial use of the University's name should be delegated to the Chancellors of each of the nine campuses. Section 9200 of the Education Code of California provides that the name of the University of California is the property of the state and no one shall use the name or any of its abbreviations on products without the permission of the Regents of the University of California. This law was originally enacted to prevent public confusion caused by misuse of the name of any of the Universities. While this was probably originally intended to prevent academic misuse, it has been extended to apply to commercial misuse. This law was recently amended to specifically include commercial products. The Chancellor of UCLA redelegated this authority to ASUCLA and any royalties which are derived from licensing of the UCLA mark are divided between UCLA and ASUCLA.

In the mid-1970s, several manufacturers came to ASUCLA and asked for the right to sell emblematic merchandise off-campus. The first license agreements on behalf of UCLA were signed with R. Gsell in 1973, P&K Products in 1974, and Artex in 1976. The salesmen for these companies recognized that they had a market for UCLA products and that was the informal start of our licensing program. We signed many other licenses in 1974 and 1975, but only the companies mentioned are still licensed. The others dropped out for one reason or another. At that time, the licenses were signed up the hill at campus administration but, shortly thereafter, they passed that responsibility down to ASUCLA, provided that the license agreement form that we used was acceptable to them.

MR: What is UCLA's licensing revenue?

Revoyr: I cannot give you an exact figure. Royalties derived from our total licensing program, including international licensing, have been quoted as being in the $400,000-$500,000 range. I think we make more money than probably any other school. Please consider the fact, however, that we do not charge a royalty for emblematic goods sold in our campus stores or to the athletic department. We only derive a royalty for sales of emblematic goods off-campus. Our position is that we are the trademark owner and user, so we do not charge our suppliers royalties. We only collect royalties for sales to non-university buyers.

MR: Where are most of your licensed products being sold?

Revoyr: Mostly in the United States and Japan. We will be signing a licensee in Canada very shortly and, if things go well, we will soon have a major program in Europe.

70% of Licensing Revenue Comes from Japan

MR: What are the demographics of your licensing program?

Revoyr: I would say that about a fifth of our total royalty-bearing, off-campus sales, are in the United States and four-fifths are international. We have 73 domestic licensees for about 24 different product categories and over 70% of our licensing revenues come from Japan.

MR: *How did you get started in Japan?*

Revoyr: In the mid-1970s a major Japanese active sportswear company called Descente came to the NCAA and said they wanted to start a licensing program in Japan that featured American colleges. So, the NCAA got into licensing by accident. They signed an agreement with Descente in 1976 to license the use of over 120 schools on a variety of clothing products. The NCAA then went around to the universities, using the contacts they knew such as the athletic directors, and got letter agreements granting the NCAA the right to license these properties. Most of the ADs lacked the authority to sign away their school's rights, but that fact was not discovered for several years. In the meantime, the money kept rolling into the various athletic departments.

It soon became apparent to Descente that they couldn't present any kind of image with 120 different schools, so they decided to pick a half dozen or so for their products. Fortunately, UCLA was one of them and we just took off. 70% of Descente's NCAA sales were UCLA products.

MR: *Why are the UCLA products so popular in Japan?*

Revoyr: I think it relates to many things. The Japanese have always had a high degree of interest in the United States, particularly in Southern California. There is an image of sunshine, beaches, golden-haired ladies, surfing, and good times. The Beach Boys were, and probably still are, huge in Japan. I think UCLA, because of its beautiful setting and location, benefitted from that perception. The idea that you could be affiliated or associated with this famous Los Angeles place appealed to a lot of people in Japan. It reached such proportions that we estimated that, at one time, the sales of licensed UCLA products in Japan were $30 million at retail.

MR: *Are sales still at that level?*

Revoyr: No. After the NCAA had the program for three years it found itself in a situation where they were paying very large royalty checks to UCLA. You can imagine what the other schools felt about UCLA getting the lion's share. I believe it put the NCAA in an awkward position. In 1979 or 1980, Descente began to develop an NCAA brand and move away from featuring any college or university. Descente created the NCAA brand by using the success of the UCLA brand. It was, in my opinion, a deliberate attempt on the part of Descente to push UCLA out of the market and replace it with NCAA and it was almost successful.

MR: *What did UCLA do?*

Revoyr: We were unable to make a direct contract with Descente although we had intended to remain with them. They were a good company and had spent a lot of money on developing the UCLA program. But we were not happy with the agreement which the NCAA had negotiated with Descente. We felt that we could have struck a better deal ourselves. The standard royalty rate in Japan is between

4-6%. After the NCAA took its share and Descente took its share for marketing expenses, our effective royalty rate from the NCAA Descente agreement was less than 2%.

MR: Are you still marketing through Descente?

Revoyr: No. We left the NCAA program after six years in 1981 and, in 1982, we signed an agreement with Renown which, I believe, is the second-largest clothing company in the world next to Levi Strauss. Whereas Descente is an active sportswear company, Renown has been a fashion company. For the last 10 or 15 years, they have carried the ARNOLD PALMER line in Japan. They decided to go into the active sportswear business and chose UCLA as a cornerstone upon which to build their activewear line. It was appropriate for both of us. While 1983 was not a good year for anyone, particularly a clothing manufacturer in Japan, the long-term prospects are very good. The Japanese economy depends to some degree on ours. While our economy started turning around last fall, theirs had not, at least yet.

MR: Are most of your licensees local to Southern California?

Revoyr: No. Only 28 of our licensees are California companies. Our biggest domestic licensee in the past had been Artex which is based in Kansas. I would think that no more than half of our domestic sales are even in Southern California. What's happened to us lately with the upcoming Summer Olympics in Los Angeles, is that a lot of the shelf space which might have been taken up with UCLA merchandise has been filled with Olympic merchandise. I think that given the past few years of business levels, a lot of buyers are being cautious and are not going to carry a wide range of collegiate licensed products. They have become quite conservative in their buying.

**** Editor's Note: According to the current ASUCLA brochure, there are more than 135 licensees worldwide for licensed UCLA products which are sold in more than 30 countries. Annual wholesale purchases by the UCLA store for such products are more than $6 million and an equal amount by other US retailers. Also, $4+ million are purchased by UCLA campus departments/groups and $6+ million by international retailers. UCLA has more than 400 trademark registrations to support its licensing program in more than 125 countries, the cost of which is $1 million in maintenance fees.

III. Successful Properties from Left Field

MICKEY MOUSE

From an interview with Pete Smith, Disney's then Executive Director of United States Merchandising in the June/July 1984 issue of *The Merchandising Reporter*.

MR: How did Disney first get involved in merchandising?

Smith: It was started by Kay Kamen, a very, very dynamic merchandising man. He was a shirt salesman from the Mid-West who would occasionally go to the movies 50 years ago or so and see the MICKEY MOUSE cartoons which preceded the feature film. He noticed the enormously enthusiastic response from the audience and got the idea of merchandising MICKEY MOUSE and other Disney characters. He hopped on a train and met with Walt and Roy Disney and sold them on the idea that he would represent them in merchandising. He had to explain to them in detail, and with considerable difficulty on his part, the idea that people would pay money to buy MICKEY MOUSE products. He ended up with worldwide rights to merchandising and publishing for all the Disney characters. Disney had just released the THREE LITTLE PIGS which had come out at the very height of the Depression and was an immediate motion picture success. That was followed by SNOW WHITE AND THE SEVEN DWARFS which was the first feature-length film in animation.

The Disney's had very high regard for Kay Kamen. After a while, however, Disney decided to get directly involved in merchandising. After the expiration of the original agreement with Kamen, Disney cut back on the rights granted to him and began to set up its own offices around the world. As it turned out, Kay was making more money than either of the Disney's. He was, unfortunately, killed in a trans-Atlantic plane crash. By contract, all the merchandising rights then reverted to the Disney organization.

MR. How have you seen licensing change from the time you first got involved?

Smith: There has been an enormous change. When I first got involved, it was difficult to explain to manufacturers and retailers that merchandising had a place. Disney was not the first. I think I found historically a character named BUSTER BROWN was the first and was merchandised by Woolworths for socks and shoes. Secondary characters of a kind, such as HOWDY DOODY and HOPALONG CASSIDY would rise and fall. Following DAVY CROCKETT, there was a whole era of westerns on television—WAGON TRAIN, BONANZA, MAVERICK. It went on and on. Most of the early ones were predictably short-lived. Every two or three years, they would rise and fall. BATMAN came and went. The BEATLES came and went. TWIGGY came and went. The Hanna Barbera characters had some continuing vitality and were cleverly and successfully merchandised by ~~Honest~~ Ed Justin. The Schultz characters, which appeared on the scene about 25 years ago, developed a wild and continuing place in American folklore and its subconsciousness. They were intelligently handled.

*****Editor's Note: According to the License Global article entitled Top 150 Global Licensors, total global sales of Disney licensed products in 2019 were $54.7 billion, which placed it as the top licensing program in the world in 2019.

PEANUTS and SNOOPY

From an interview with Mike Georgopolis, the then SVP Licensing for United Media Enterprises in the June/July 1984 issue of *The Merchandising Reporter*.

MR: How did SNOOPY first get involved in merchandising? Was it a conscious decision on the part of Mr. Schultz or was it just a situation where someone approached him and said, "Hey, can I have a license for T-Shirts?"

Georgopolis: It goes back a couple of decades with Holt-Rinehart who had published a comic strip collection. From that publication, a simple idea was generated by one very strong and determined individual, Connie Boucher, who was the principal at Determined Productions and who was the First Lady of character merchandising.

She had a notion that a cute little dog might be saleable to the consumer. At just about that same time, we also had the opportunity to prepare an animated television special for CBS and, through the talents and imagination of Mr. Schulz and the experience of its producer, Lee Mendelson, and Bill Melendez, the brilliant animator, we went on the air in 1965 with our first special. Since then, we have had about two dozen more specials, and the licensing program has grown to involve licenses in hundreds of merchandise categories.

MR: How extensively is SNOOPY being licensed?

GEORGOPOLIS: We approve 200 products a month here on the PEANUTS property and we have several hundred licensees. SNOOPY products appear in virtually every free world market.

CABBAGE PATCH KIDS

The CABBAGE PATCH Kids were a line of soft sculptured dolls initially created and sold by Xavier Roberts, then a 21-year-old art student. He said that he had utilized the quilting skills that he learned from his mother along with the technique of "needle molding" to develop his line of fabric sculptures. These hand-stitched, one-of-a-kind, soft fabric sculptures were called LITTLE PEOPLE. He registered some of his early designs in the Copyright Office in 1978.

Many of the defining characteristics of the LITTLE PEOPLE, including the dolls' overly round faces, were similar to a product called DOLL BABIES that had been marketed by Martha Nelson Thomas, an American folk artist from Kentucky. She and Xavier Roberts had supposedly crossed paths at a state fair in 1976.

Roberts employed a marketing gimmick in catching the public's attention. The LITTLE PEOPLE were not offered for sale but, rather, were "adopted," complete with their own name and birth certificate. Instead of paying a purchase price, buyers paid an "adoption fee."

The LITTLE PEOPLE dolls were initially marketed at arts and craft shows and then at Babyland General Hospital in Cleveland, GA, a former medical clinic that Roberts had converted into a toy store. Babyland General Hospital was complete with a birthing room, nursery, and adoption center for the CABBAGE PATCH Kids. Employees dressed and acted as doctors and nurses caring for the dolls as if they were real babies. In 2010, Babyland General was eventually moved into a new facility on the outskirts of Cleveland, Georgia, which has been named as one of the Travel Channel's Top 10 Toyland's.

Some of the early transactions involving the LITTLE PEOPLE are noteworthy. The first LITTLE PEOPLE "quintuplets" were sold for $5000 to a couple from Cummings, GA and one of Roberts' first-ever dolls was sold at auction in the 1980s for $3000.

The LITTLE PEOPLE were renamed the CABBAGE PATCH Kids with great fanfare as reported in *Newsweek*, *The Wall Street Journal*, and the *Atlanta Weekly*.

The visibility and popularity of the property exploded when Roberts' company, Original Appalachian Artworks, signed a master toy license with Coleco

 Toys in August 1982 for a smaller version of the product and Coleco began mass-producing them. The Coleco license agreement was negotiated by Roger Schlaifer of Schlaifer-Nance & Company who would then become the exclusive, worldwide, licensing agent for Roberts.

Coleco introduced the CABBAGE PATCH Kids with a splash at the 1983 International Toy Fair in New York. By October, riots were occurring in stores

around the country because of a shortage of the dolls amid great demand. The dolls were featured on the cover of *Newsweek* before Christmas and stories of their success spread around the world.

At its peak, CABBAGE PATCH dolls were a must-have toy for Christmas, and parents lined up outside of retailers to be able to purchase the dolls for their children. Its retail selling price in 1983 was $30, but black-market versions were sold for as much as $75. Every doll also came with Roberts' signature on its butt.

In addition to the Coleco license, Schlaifer Nance signed more than 150 licensees for a host of licensed products, including character diapers, board games, cereal, clothing, backyard pools, animated cartoons, etc., which surpassed $2 billion in retail sales for 1984.

The CABBAGE PATCH licensing program also branched out to both music and video. The CD, entitled *CABBAGE PATCH Dreams*, produced by the Chapin Brothers for Parker Brothers' music, went Gold and Platinum in 1983, and the video game *CABBAGE PATCH Kids: Adventures in the Park* video game was released that same year.

The total sales of licensed CABBAGE PATCH products generated by Schlaifer Nance were more than $4.5 billion.

Coleco originally manufactured the dolls in a factory in Amsterdam, NY before production moved to Asia. Nine head variations were produced which were computer matched to the bodies to ensure that each doll was "different." This proved to be a successful marketing technique. Some of the companies that manufactured the dolls abroad included Lili Ledy Toy Company who made the dolls for Mexico and South America; Triang-Pedigree Toy Company who made the dolls for South Africa; and Tsukuda Toy Company who manufactured the dolls for Japan and Asia.

When Coleco went bankrupt in 1988, Hasbro took over the rights and continued to make the dolls with various additions, etc. including "Birthday Kids", "Splash 'n' Tan Kids", and "Pretty Crimp and Curl." Hasbro gradually began making the dolls for younger children, which led to smaller and smaller dolls.

In 1994, Mattel acquired the licensing rights and the first Mattel version coming out in 1995. The Mattel dolls were mostly sized 14" or smaller and most were individualized to enhance their collectability. Some of the Mattel CABBAGE PATCH dolls were made to coincide with the 1996 Olympics and the CABBAGE PATCH Fairies. To celebrate the dolls' 15th anniversary, Mattel created a line of exclusively female dolls with a new molded fabric face, dressed in custom outfits and packaged in collectible boxes.

Other licensees after Mattel included Toys "R" Us; Play Along Toys (both alone and by JAKKS Pacific after it acquired Play Along); and finally Wicked Cool Toys, the current toy licensee.

The CABBAGE PATCH doll was one of the most popular toy fads of the 1980s and one of the longest-running doll franchises in the United States.

Xavier Roberts was no stranger to litigation. Martha Nelson Thomas maintained that Roberts had taken the concept of CABBAGE PATCH Kids from her, and she brought a suit against Roberts, eventually settling with him for an undisclosed amount in 1985. Thomas maintained that she was more concerned by the corruption of her dolls than the money she may have lost.

Roberts brought a $30 million lawsuit against Topps for copyright infringement based on their marketing parody trading cards called the GARBAGE PAIL KIDS. Topps eventually settled by agreeing to cease parodying the CABBAGE PATCH Kids.

TEENAGE MUTANT NINJA TURTLES

The TEENAGE MUTANT NINJA TURTLES ("TMNT") are four, fictional, teen-aged anthropomorphic TURTLES named after Italian Renaissance artists who were allegedly trained in the art of *ninjutsu*. From the sewers of New York City, they battle petty criminals, evil overlords, mutated creatures, and alien invaders while attempting to remain hidden from society.

The TURTLES were created in 1983 by Kevin Eastman and Peter Laird, two then struggling artists from Northampton, MA. Literally, as a joke, Eastman drew a turtle standing on its hind legs, wearing a mask with nunchucks strapped to its arms and wrote "Ninja Turtle" on the top of the page. The pair laughed and then Laird drew a more refined version of the turtle. Eastman then drew four TURTLES, each armed with a ninja-style weapon. Laird outlined the group shot in ink and added "Teenage Mutant" to the "NINJA TURTLES" title. Thus, the TEENAGE MUTANT NINJA TURTLES were born.

Since the pair envisioned creating a comic book, they needed to name the individual TURTLES characters, choosing the names of great Renaissance artists— Leonardo, Raphael, Donatello, and Michelangelo.

Eastman and Lair launched their first comic book in May 1984 at a comic book convention in Portsmouth, NH under the banner of Mirage Studios—based on their not having an actual studio. They placed a full-page ad in Comic Buyer's Guide #547 which caught the attention of the public and the phenomenon began.

Mirage sold all the original 3,000 copies that they printed within a few weeks. The second printing of 6,000 copies followed, which also quickly sold. That put Eastman and Laird into the black.

The TURTLES created their own language, borrowing surfer lingo such as "bummer," "dude," "bogus," "radical," "far-out," "tubuloso," and "bodacious." Their most recognized phrase was "cowabunga."

Mirage Studios published regular issues of the comics from 1984 to 1995, in addition to mini-series and limited editions. Archie Comics published 72 issues of the "Adventures" series between 1988 and 1995 under license from Mirage.

In June 1996, Image Comics took over publishing, commencing with volume 3 of the series which was a slightly more, action-oriented TMNT series. Mirage resumed publishing in 2001 and continued until 2007 when it went on "indefinite hiatus." It would continue intermittent publishing through 2014.

A daily comic strip began in 1990, featuring an adventure story Monday through Friday and activity puzzles on weekends. The comic strip remained in syndication until its cancellation in December 1996. At its highest point in popularity, it was published in over 250 newspapers.

The TURTLES phenomenon started when a licensing agent, Mark Freedman, sought out the artists and proposed wider merchandising opportunities. In January 1987, they visited Playmates Toys, a small California toy company that wanted to expand into the action-figure market. Playmates got excited about the prospect and put together a creative team that would ultimately produce an animated mini-series that lasted for 10 seasons.

In 1990, a live-action feature film was released, with the TURTLES portrayed by actors in partially animatronic suits created by Jim Henson's Creature Shop. The film spawned two sequels. After the end of the animated series, a live-action series in the vein of the films was created in 1997 in conjunction with Saban Entertainment.

In 1997–1998, the TURTLES starred in a live-action television series called *NINJA TURTLES: The Next Mutation* that directly followed the events of the first three movies. In 2003, a new TMNT series produced by 4Kids Entertainment and co-produced by Mirage Studios began airing on the "Fox Box" (later renamed "4Kids TV") programming block. It later moved to "The CW4Kids" block. This series lasted until 2009, ending with a feature-length television movie titled *TURTLES Forever*, which was produced in conjunction with the 25th anniversary of the TMNTs franchise and featured the TURTLES of the 2003 series teaming up with their counterparts from the 1987 series.

Nickelodeon acquired the global rights to TEENAGE MUTANT NINJA TURTLES and announced a new CGI-animated TMNT television series which ran for five seasons. Nickelodeon announced a new 2D animated series based on the franchise, which debuted on September 17, 2018.

All told, the TURTLES have appeared in six feature films beginning in the early 1990s: *TEENAGE MUTANT NINJA TURTLES* (1990), *TEENAGE MUTANT NINJA TURTLES II: The Secret of the Ooze* (1991), and *TEENAGE MUTANT NINJA TURTLES III* (1993). The fourth film, a CGI-animated film called *TMNT*, was released in 2007. A reboot, also titled *TEENAGE MUTANT NINJA TURTLES* was released in 2014 and a sequel titled *TEENAGE MUTANT NINJA TURTLES: Out of the Shadows* was released in 2016. A seventh film, which is another reboot, is in development.

At the height of the frenzy in the late 1980s and early 1990s, the TURTLES' likenesses could be found on a wide range of children's merchandise, from PEZ dispensers to skateboards, breakfast cereal, video games, school supplies, linens, towels, cameras, and toy shaving kits.

Among the first licensed products featuring the TMNT characters was a tabletop role-playing game published by Palladium Books in 1985 and featuring original comics and illustrations by Eastman and Laird. In 1986, Dark Horse Miniatures in Boise, Idaho, produced a set of licensed lead figurines. The franchise generated merchandise sales of $175 million in 1988 and $350 million in 1989. By 1994, it was the most merchandisable franchise, having generated total revenue of $6 billion in merchandise sales up until then.

From 1988 – 1997, Playmates produced 400 or more TURTLES action figures, as well as dozens of vehicles and playsets. For the first four years of TURTLE mania, about $1.1 billion worth of toys were sold, making the TURTLES the #3 top-selling toy figures ever at the time, behind only G.I. JOE and STAR WARS. Playmates produced a series of TMNT/STAR TREK crossover figures, due to Playmates holding the STAR TREK action-figure license at the time. Never in toy history did an action-figure line have such an impact for over two decades, generating billions of dollars in licensing revenue.

The TURTLES were also heavily licensed in the video game market. The first console video game based on the franchise, entitled *TEENAGE MUTANT NINJA TURTLES*, was released under the "Ultra Games" label in 1989 and was later converted to home computers and, eventually, the Wii. In 2006, Ubisoft acquired the rights for TMNT games, along with a game for the Game Boy Advance similar in style to the Nintendo arcade games.

During the height of their popularity, the TURTLES also had several food tie-ins. Among the most notable of these products was NINJA TURTLES Cereal, produced by Ralston-Purina which came with a small pouch of Pizza CRUNCHABUNGAS—pizza-flavored corn snacks in the shape of pizzas; HOSTESS NINJA TURTLES Pudding Pies, featuring a green sugar crust and vanilla pudding inside; and ROYAL OOZE Gelatin Desserts, distributed by Nabisco.

A TURTLES concert tour was held in 1990 featuring live-action TURTLES playing music as a band. It launched at Radio City Music Hall, and a pay-per-view special was later broadcast. In 1990, the TMNT characters appeared in the "New York Street" section of Disney-MGM Studios theme park in Orlando, Florida.

Nickelodeon Universe at American Dream Meadowlands in New Jersey, which opened in 2019, contains several TMNT-themed rides, including two coasters that broke world records upon their opening.

As one would expect of a successful property, it was the subject of litigation. Eastman and Laird were sued for $5 million by Buffalo Bob Smith, host of the *HOWDY DOODY Show*, who claimed they stole "Cowabunga!" from his program. The word was first used as the catchphrase greeting of a Native American character named CHIEF THUNDERTHUD. It had, however, been adopted by surfers in the 1960s. After a few months of legal wrangling, Smith settled for $50,000.

How Licensees Discovered PAC-MAN

From a 1983 interview in the *Merchandising Reporter* with Stan Jarocki of Bally-Midway.

MR: Was PAC-MAN Bally Midway's first venture into licensing?

JAROCKI: It started as a small thing, going back to the summer of 1981 when video games first became a formidable form of entertainment in the United States. Our

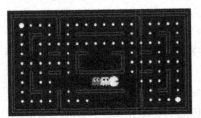

advertising specialty suppliers began to get interest from the public in items we produced to promote our new games to the trade. Arcade managers wanted to sell these items to promote the new games in their locations. This beginning of licensing for sales promotion started with SPACE INVADERS and GALAXIAN and spread like wildfire with PAC-MAN. Other companies became interested in PAC-MAN and the list of licensed products skyrocketed.

MR: How did Bally Midway first get involved with PAC-MAN?

JAROCKI: We licensed it from Namco Limited. I went to Japan in mid-August of 1980 at the invitation of Namco and saw four games at the Japanese Amusement Show. One of the games that was very interesting was PAC-MAN, which turned out to be the strongest of the four games that we saw. We brought it to the United States and introduced it as a coin-operated video game in November 1980 at the Amusement and Music Operators' Association Show in Chicago. The game was virtually an immediate success because, although other maze/chase games were introduced in the industry in the past, none had been successful. I guess the success was because of the cuteness of the PAC-MAN character and the non-violence of the game, it's not a shoot 'em up type of game. It is a low-key, fun game to play. You do not have to be a macho type to play the game. PAC-MAN is universal; anyone can play and enjoy it. Previously, games had been designed for macho type players. PAC-MAN is popular with all age groups and both sexes. This appeal allowed it to be placed in nearly any location. Market penetration has been phenomenal, and this has, again, enhanced the popularity of the character.

MR: *What type of arrangement do you have with Namco?*

JAROCKI: We have the rights to exclusively manufacture and market the game in the Western Hemisphere. We also get rights in other parts of the world. The audio-visual works of the game have been copyrighted with the U.S. Copyright Office.

MR: *Who named it PAC-MAN?*

JAROCKI: The game in Japan was originally called Puck-Man. We felt that the name was not right for the United States because you have all the graffiti writers and it would have been too easy for them to take and damage or destroy the game by the change of a letter on the game. So, for our purposes, we had the name changed to PAC-MAN. Bally Midway owns the rights to the mark PAC-MAN as well as to the character.

MR: *Who decided to get involved with the PAC MAN game in the first place?*

JAROCKI: Well I saw it for the company and discussed it with our management because I felt that it had strong possibilities in our marketplace. There was a need for a change in the game concept in the United States. The success of the SPACE INVADERS game brought on a whole series of space-oriented, shoot 'em up games. We needed a change of pace to take that edge off space games. Then here came PAC-MAN. It was a very simple game to play. We were looking to increase the player base, which is very important in our industry. If we were to continue to grow and have new players play our video games for the first time, we had to have something new and different and we had to get more people involved. The best place to tap was the female players who were, in a sense, inhibited by games like SPACE INVADERS and GALAXIAN. They played driving games and sports games, but not to any great extent. But when PAC-MAN came along, it just grabbed everybody. I think one of the reasons for its success was due to the popularity with the female player base.

MR: Has Bally Midway ever taken an active role in seeking licensees?

JAROCKI: At the beginning of our licensing experience, many people came to us seeking PAC-MAN licenses. Since that time, we have taken a very active role in seeking out prospective licensees for all our other popular video game properties. We have a game called DOMINO MAN which introduced a whole new series of characters; a game called SOLAR FOX, a space-oriented game introducing a female space person. For games like BURGER TIME and others, we have created the characters with merchandising in mind. When we introduce games to our trade, prospective licensees  become interested in those properties, again for T-shirts and other high turnover items. Because we intend to expand our licensing department, we have been adding staff to a fine nucleus headed by JoAnn Sutherland.

A Yarn about Pom Poms on Tennis Socks

One of Greg Battersby's favorite stories from when he working as a patent attorney at Gulf + Western Industries in the early 1980s involved his work with Kayser-Roth Hosiery, one of G+W's companies. Kayser-Roth Hosiery had been approached by a small hosiery mill that held the patent rights to an invention that was intended to prevent a tennis half-sock from sliding down during play.

This was a time when the elastic yarns used today were still in the process of development, and it was not uncommon for non-elastic socks to slip down into the heel of a wearer's sneaker or tennis shoe during play. With the advent and development of elastic yarns, that problem became a thing of the past.

In any event, the owner of a small hosiery mill was tasked by his tennis-playing wife with coming up with a way to prevent her socks from slipping down during play. As he recalls the situation, the hosiery mill was very small, and the owner was very concerned about being able to eventually fund his retirement ... let alone keeping his wife in tennis lessons and gameplay.

What he came up with was an ingenious (at the time) approach to the problem. He attached a simple "pom-pom" to the back of the sock in the heel area which prevented the sock from slipping during use. He sought and obtained patent protection for the idea. Not only was it functional, but it was decorative, and soon became the rage of the tennis-playing set, so much so, that virtually every hosiery company, including Kayser-Roth Hosiery, was interested in taking a license under the patent.

The revenues that it generated enabled him and his wife to cease worry about their retirement. He knows this because the inventor came back a year or so later and asked whether he knew which banks were paying the best rate of return on certificates of deposits of at least $100,000 (a lot of money in those days). He also asked Greg for advice about product extensions, but he recalls telling him that once you have developed the best thing since sliced bread, it is hard to improve on that.

Larkins on Licensing in Japan

This is an excerpt from Ted Larkins' book entitled *Get to Be Happy* which he described as a "life-changing" event in his licensing career in Japan.

Here's another life-changing moment that, much like learning the language, has defined my life ever since. At 10 o'clock one night about five months into the homestay, Yoshida knocked on my bedroom door, looked at me, and said, "We do big business." Yoshida owned a small electronics import-export company. I said, "Sure, let's do big business." Whatever that meant.

He came in, sat down (on a cushion on the floor, of course), and handed me a small, ripped piece of paper with a phone number on it. He said, "I use JAMES DEAN on T-shirts. You call the number."

Huh? But whatever. So, I picked up the phone, dialed the number, and someone answered.

I said, "Hi there. My name is Ted, and I'm here in Japan with a guy who wants to use a photo of JAMES DEAN on T-shirts. He gave me this number to call. Can you help?"

The guy on the other end of the line said, "Sure, my name is Marcus Winslow, I'm James' cousin. How much do you think you're going to sell?"

In my better (but still terrible) Japanese I asked Yoshida. He told me, and I said to Marcus, "About $100,000 in sales." "Okay," Marcus replied, "Pay me 10% of that, which is called a royalty by the way, and I'll send you some photos to use. I'll have my agent send you a contract tomorrow." And that's how it started.

His agents, Beth and Mark, were Godsends, especially Beth, who taught me the ins and outs of "licensing"—the business of taking names, images, and logos, and putting them on products to sell. The contract came via fax that rolled up as it came out of the machine, which I then had to tear into separate pages with a ruler. Yoshida signed it and we sent it back to Marcus with a check for $10,000. A week later an envelope arrived with photos of JAMES DEAN and Yoshida's company, Sunworld, started selling JAMES DEAN T-shirts.

A month later, Yoshida stopped by my room again and said, "Call him back. We want to make baseball caps." JAMES DEAN baseball caps? Really? So, I did, and for an extra $3,000, we added baseball caps to the contract. So, it went: every few weeks Yoshida would stop by, I would call Beth, and we would add more products to the contract. Although still bartending, I started working a couple of days a week at Yoshida's office in the city facilitating communications.

Yoshida at one point stopped by a desk I had now been given, looked at the pile of papers all splayed on top, and stated simply, "You file." I filed, setting up a rinky-dink system of tracking the contracts and other things I was doing. I had a typewriter to type letters—and lots of Whiteout. I got a book on typing and learned how.

And you know what happened? Over the next five years, while I was still bartending, teaching English, and otherwise having a Get To life in Japan, Sunworld sold more than $80 million in JAMES DEAN products: shirts, hats, shoes, sunglasses, bags, socks, towels, ski-boot tote bags, and a myriad of other things. We paid Marcus over $4 million in royalties. This unfolding of life, we just do not know. What I do know, however, is that I was having a blast.

****

In March of 1994, now becoming more fluent in Japanese, I was introduced to Jonathan Zilli, a Senior Vice President of Paramount Pictures. We set a meeting in the lobby of a London hotel and, when we met, he said, "Call me JZ." I thought, *I'm a bartender and I get to call a movie studio executive JZ. How cool is that?* He said, "I heard you've been doing licensing for PEPSI in Japan."

"Yes," I said tentatively, "and?"

"Well, we own the movies STAR TREK, TOP GUN, THE GODFATHER, and most of the Audrey Hepburn films such as ROMAN HOLIDAY, SABRINA, and BREAKFAST AT TIFFANY'S. Could you guys sell stuff with those movie images on them?"

I didn't think so, but I said, "Of course."

I returned to Japan and a faxed contract appointing us as the "agent" for Paramount Pictures in Japan soon arrived. By this time, Yoshida and the guys were pretty good at putting JAMES DEAN's face and the PEPSI logo on things, but they had no idea what to do with a movie title. At first, they were excited about the prospect of putting a picture of Tom Cruise from the movie TOP GUN on a T-shirt to sell. When the Paramount attorney saw it, however, he freaked out. The fax from Paramount's legal department was clear, "You can't use Tom Cruise's image on products!"

Enter Sunamori, a friend of Yoshida's who was renting a desk in our building and had his own marketing company. Sunamori said he could do some deals, even without Tom Cruise or other actor images. A month later he came into the office and said, "Hey, I got a deal from a company that wants to turn ROMAN HOLIDAY"—the 1953 film that won several Academy Awards, including Best Actress for Audrey Hepburn—"into a stage play."

"Wow," I said, "that's cool. How much will they pay for the right to do that?"

"A million dollars!" *What?* So, I began negotiating a million-dollar deal for a Broadway-type stage play in Tokyo. It was a two-year negotiation (negotiating with the Japanese is a story unto itself), but in the end, the play was a huge success in Japan, generating millions of dollars to Paramount in rights royalties. It was time to quit my bartending job.

Given our success with Paramount, many studios began calling me to ask if we would represent their films, TV shows, or artists, and for the next 15 years. We did. Yoshida's Sunworld company focused on PEPSI, NEW BALANCE, JAMES DEAN, and other "brands." Until his crash and burn (a tragic tale I'll share), Sunamori's division of Sunworld, Sun R & P, focused on entertainment. We became the agent for Sony Pictures and Sony Music, including the films GHOSTBUSTERS, MEN IN BLACK, and SPIDER-MAN, the classic TV library for BEWITCHED and I DREAM OF JEANNIE, and music-artist greats such as MARIAH CAREY, CELINE DION, KISS, and MICHAEL JACKSON.

We represented MGM Studios and their films PINK PANTHER, ROCKY, MEN IN BLACK, and ROBOCOP; 20th Century Fox's TV shows 24 and THE SIMPSONS, as well as their films AVATAR, ALIEN, and PLANET OF THE APES; CBS's STAR TREK; and DreamWorks' SHREK and KUNG FU PANDA.

We did deals for Hollywood-themed arcades, stage plays for RAIN MAN, GHOST, and ZORRO, a cosmetic line for AUDREY HEPBURN, an apparel line for GRACE KELLY, the BRUCE LEE attraction I had gone to visit when my Dad died, and multimillion-dollar PACHINKO deals (*pachinko* are slot machines in Japan) for dozens of films. Over the years, the projects Sunworld did generate hundreds of millions of dollars in product sales in Japan.

You will forgive me if in this instance I don't use *Get To—Smile—Do it!* but simply say, "What the hell? This life is so crazy! And it was about to get crazier." By the way, people were starting to make fun of my Osaka-ben—and I was in heaven!

Carole Postal's Postings

I have been involved in the licensing industry for over 35 years. I participated in the first-ever Licensing Show, such as it was, with such stalwart heroes in our universe ... Danny Simon and Shirley Henschel. And there were so many others. Who remembers the Atlantic City Licensing Show back in 1984? Karen Spitz and Ita Golzman do! And of course, so do I! I was there representing RIPLEY'S BELIEVE IT OR NOT! Nope, I cannot believe it! There are so many memories to recall going back so many years!!! Of course, I was a mere child ... and still am! This crazy world of licensing keeps us young in heart and spirit. It is only the body and technology that make us feel old. When a three-year-old knows how to do something you cannot! But not licensing for sure!

There are so many wonderful stories to share about how things came about in terms of licensing opportunities back then. Launching a character called IT'S HAPPY BUNNY for tweens and teens back in the late '90s when nobody marketed properties to those target age groups, except, of course, the retailer HOT TOPIC! Three-quarters of a billion dollars later in retail sales over ten years, believe me, nobody was laughing then. The naysayers screamed how can you market a character that is not on TV or in the movies! Everybody laughed. But, as ever in this fickle world of licensing, everybody started jumping on the tween bandwagon—property owners, manufacturers, retailers—but we started it with a creator, Jim Benton, and his creation "a little bunny that said naughty things" and some licensing agent moxie! It was a win/win and started a whole new licensing category: trend licensing! Those were the fun years!

But licensing also represents love stories. My husband, Vice Chairman of Mayfair Industries (later publicly traded as Apparel America), Robert Postal, walked into my office in 1989 at MGM/UA and never left. We married two years later and stayed happily married for 27 years until he died nearly 5 years ago. The interest that brought him to my offices at MGM was in licensing the 50th Anniversary of THE WIZARD OF OZ for apparel and working with MACY'S, who was re-creating the magic of the MGM movie in a store. Yellow brick roads led consumers to ruby slippers for sale and apparel with brilliant red, yellow, and green for the Emerald City emblazoned on garments. Oh my, the sheer breadth of the magic that MACY'S created in-store will go down in the annals of retail history. 5,500 tap dancers bedecked in beloved apparel from the film and tap dancing in ruby red slippers down Broadway leading up MACY'S in Herald Square was something to behold. Those were the days! Magic was recreated in real time and in product!

One of my favorite stories was launching a teen lifestyle brand called PINK COOKIE, which started as a sock! Yes, a sock! Not a TV show, a movie, a comic strip, nor an impresario hawking infomercial. Just a sock!

PINK COOKIE was a made-up brand with creativity and artwork so unique and in tune with its customer base that it landed on retail shelves as hosiery and blew out of every mid-tier national chain in which it was displayed for sale. From there we licensed apparel, stationery, social expression, home goods … in short, everything that could complete a teen's PINK COOKIE lifestyle. And the sheer beauty of the brand was that there were no marketing funds behind it nor a famous spokesperson. Just a fabulous artist/head salesperson/owner, Tony Aloia of HYP, and his sheer creativity and salesmanship! My team and Tony created a global brand that spoke to the teen and young adult customer that wanted to be that PINK COOKIE girl. Again, a combination of creativity and licensing moxie that set our little piece of the universe on fire!

And then, more recently, was our licensing of a Masterpiece Theater, target audience 65 and older, limited television series entitled DOWNTON ABBEY. Who could license a period piece drama based on an Edwardian era family, not based on any book series but the source material written for a TV show???!!! Everybody laughed and laughed.

I saw the show in London before it launched in America and my good friend Steve Manners, then VP of what was then Copyright Promotions, recommended me for the licensing agent in America and 45+ licensees later, and thousands of licensed products … another licensing success story was born! And there were so many naysayers. For two years everyone said it was impossible. 65+ persons did not represent the core competency of buying licensed products! Who knew that the ultimate success of the show and the licensed product would lend themselves to generations of buyers, everyone coming together to enjoy 6 seasons of the show and a full-length feature film! The success of the licensing and the retail sales of the licensed product continues. Through the generous support of the Executive Producer, Gareth Neame, and his team, the show has been an absolute joy to work on in terms of licensing. Another licensing story about everyone saying it cannot be done!!!

The moral to these stories above is that there is no playbook for licensing. Sometimes licensing magic works because the stars align, sometimes it is the right timing and the right people together with the right chemistry, and sometimes it is just meant to be. Perhaps it is the luck of the Irish or, maybe, just good old-fashioned know-how and the guts to make it happen! I don't know. But it is the beauty of our licensing world that keeps the freshness and creativity moving forward and sometimes the littlest idea or Facebook friend, can become the biggest licensing sensation.

Just look at BOO, THE WORLD'S CUTEST DOG, the first animal Social Media sensation and one of the best -selling plushes from GUND. You gotta' love this crazy world of licensing. I do, Greg does, and I hope you do too!

IV. The Road Less Traveled

IBM Licenses DOS Not CPM

There are many stories, some true, some partially true and some pure fiction, about the origins of the original license deal between Bill Gates and Paul Allen and their company, Microsoft, and IBM involving the development and use MS-DOS as the operating system for the original IBM Personal Computer in the early 1980s. The operating system, or "OS" as it's called, is the foundational software for a computer. It permits computers to function. Without it, a computer is simply a collection of electronic components with no useful purpose.

At the time IBM was developing its first PC in the late 1970s and early 1980s, IBM was mostly into large, mainframe computers and business machines such as the Selectric typewriter and memory typewriter lines. IBM's PC project was a low-priority, low budget project intended mainly to fill out its product line with a desktop microcomputer. Management didn't expect the product, or for that matter, the desktop microcomputer to become the industry that it would ultimately become. Their primary competition at the time was the start-up, Apple Computer, with its Apple][computer which had been introduced in 1977 as well as the Commodore Pet and Tandy microcomputers.

While IBM was certainly capable of developing its own operating system and had done so for many of its larger systems, it decided to use third-party software for its PC, including a third-party operating system. The purpose was to keep project costs low and permit them to meet delivery schedules.

At the time, the most advanced microcomputer operating system on the market was a system called CP/M (Control Program for Microprocessors) which had been developed by Gary Kildall, a Ph.D. computer instructor who ran a company called Digital Research. More than 600,000 copies of CP/M had been sold at the time, and it set the industry standard.

CP/M differed from other operating systems of the day in that it relied on English-like commands to the chip instead of using the 0s and 1s which was the standard at that time. CP/M became the dominant microcomputer operating system of the 1970s, powering machines from Xerox, Kaypro, Kentucky Fried Computers, and Morrow.

Microsoft Team

When IBM was finally ready to consider an operating system for its PC, its first stop was Microsoft and Bill Gates, since IBM already had an NDA in place with them to deliver an 8086 BASIC interpreter for the IBM PC. The IBM PC project was very hush-hush, and IBM wanted to carefully limit the number of third parties to those parties who were already covered by an NDA. So, it made sense for them to approach a software vendor such as Microsoft with whom it had already been working on the PC project.

When they approached Gates about supplying the entire operating system, his initial response was that Microsoft didn't do operating systems, particularly after IBM told him that they wanted their operating system to look like CP/M. Gates referred the IBM representatives to Gary Kildall at Digital Research. Gates then let Kildall know that some important (but undisclosed) folks wanted to talk with him. Since Gates had signed an NDA with IBM, he couldn't share the details of the visit or what they wanted.

History is a little fuzzy about exactly what happened next, but it appears that IBM did approach Digital Research about CP/M, and some combination of the following events occurred which prevented the parties from making a deal:

- Digital Research was hesitant to sign the IBM NDA, which was required before the IBM PC project could even be discussed;
- Kildall was not available when IBM representatives attempted to meet with him initially ... legend has it he was either out fishing or flying his plane and/or was late for the meeting;
- While Kildall had done some work on an 8086 version of CP/M, it was not very far along, so there would have been a delay in getting a fully implemented and tested version for the PC; and/or
- Digital Research and IBM could not agree on the financial terms of a deal for CP/M, allegedly because Kildall was asking for a flat fee over $200,000 which was more than IBM was reportedly willing to pay.

Unable to conclude a deal with Kildall and feeling frustrated, the IBM representatives resumed discussions with Microsoft. The parties then met to discuss the state of Microsoft's work on home computers and explore what Microsoft could do for IBM. Gates gave IBM a few ideas on what would make a great home computer, among them to have Basic written into the ROM chip. Microsoft had already produced several versions of Basic for different computer systems beginning with the Altair, so Gates was more than happy to write a version for IBM.

The IBM representatives liked what they heard and began to negotiate a license agreement with Gates.

One thing standing in the way of that agreement, however, was that Microsoft first needed to acquire rights to an operating system called QDOS (for

"Quick and Dirty Operating System") which was also called 86-DOS. 86-DOS had been written by Tim Paterson of Seattle Computer Products ("SCP"). Gates knew about 86-DOS and discussed it with IBM. Legend has it that that 86-DOS was based on Gary Kildall's CP/M and that Tim Paterson had supposedly bought a CP/M manual and used it as the basis to write his operating system in six weeks. Peterson, of course, vehemently denied this charge.

Gates suggested that IBM could try to get 86-DOS from SCP, but IBM was not interested in getting involved with yet another software vendor, given how things had gone with Digital Research. It preferred to work with Microsoft. IBM suggested that Microsoft acquire the rights to the 86-DOS software, port it to the IBM PC hardware, and license it to IBM for the PC. Microsoft agreed and went ahead to purchase the rights to 86-DOS from SCP, reportedly for $25K. They would also hire Peterson to work on the IBM project.

That set the stage for the eventual license between Microsoft and IBM which would eventually propel Microsoft to one of the world's largest and most profitable companies. Recognizing the potential for MS-DOS, Gates agreed to give IBM a non-exclusive license for an initial fee well below what IBM was prepared to pay. In exchange, Microsoft wanted to retain the right to license the software to other computer manufacturers. The non-exclusive nature of the grant and the ability to ultimately license their operating system as MS-DOS to the exploding PC market turned out to be a stroke of genius for Microsoft. Gates and IBM then concluded the deal and the rest is history.

On August 12, 1981, IBM introduced its new revolution in a box, the "Personal Computer," complete with a brand new, 16-bit, Microsoft computer operating system called PC-DOS 1.0 which would become the heart and soul of the personal computer market. Microsoft created two versions of DOS. One was known as PC-DOS, which was specifically for the IBM PC. Microsoft retained the rights to sell its own version of DOS, known as MS-DOS, for all the PC clones not manufactured by IBM.

Kildall did not take the news well. He became bitter, claiming that MS-DOS copied the best features of CP/M with enough differences to make it incompatible with CP/M. He threatened to sue Gates and Microsoft but never did. What particularly bothered Kildall was that he found himself having to compete in the IBM compatible market with a clone of his work called DR-DOS which never dented Microsoft's sales.

Novell would ultimately buy Kildall's firm in 1991, but it was never able to make much money with it. Ironically, a few years later, Microsoft agreed to sanctions imposed by the Justice Department over how it had licensed MS-DOS during the period that Kildall was trying to get traction with DR-DOS.

On July 6, 1994, Kildall, then 54, walked into a Monterey biker bar wearing motorcycle leather with Harley-Davidson patches, got into an altercation with some of the bikers, and ultimately died from the injuries he sustained.

The morale of the story—don't take the day off to go fishing.

STAR WARS—If You Can't Buy it, Create Your Own

A long time ago in a galaxy far, far away...

George Lucas, the creator of the STAR WARS property, was a big fan of a television series called *Adventure Theater* which featured FLASH GORDON. The story is that he tried to buy the rights to that series and character to fulfill a boyhood dream of creating a B-movie hero, but he failed. So, Lucas decided to craft a serial adventure of his own, set in space against the backdrop of civil war. He borrowed from Edgar Rice Burroughs (JOHN CARTER OF MARS); from Akira Kurosawa (THE HIDDEN FORTRESS), and World War II dog fights to create a far-away galaxy filled with colorful characters that evoked the romantic thrills of antique adventures.

The early development of the original STAR WARS motion picture proved difficult for Lucas. He wrote a short space fantasy film summary but was frustrated that his story was too difficult to understand. After finishing the film AMERICAN GRAFITTI, he began writing a 13-page treatment for STAR WARS and expanded the treatment into a rough draft screenplay.

Efforts to sell the screenplay to United Artists were unsuccessful. Universal also passed, as did Disney. Finally, Alan Ladd, Jr. at Fox agreed to finance the film, primarily to develop a relationship with Lucas whose picture, AMERICAN GRAFITTI, had been Oscar-nominated. Ladd reportedly told Lucas, "I don't understand this, but I loved AMERICAN GRAFITTI, and whatever you do is okay with me." Lucas later said that if it hadn't been for Fox, he didn't believe that the STAR WARS films would have ever been made.

They settled on an $8 million budget (less than the cost of a Bond film at the time), and Lucas went to Tunisia. But before he got there, however, Lucas made what might be the best business decision in Hollywood history. When AMERICAN GRAFITTI became one of the most profitable films of all time during its mid-70s theatrical run, Lucas was encouraged to re-negotiate his directorial fee for STAR WARS from $150,000 to $500,000. His star was on the rise and he may have been able to do it, but he didn't. Instead, he told Fox he was willing to take his original director's fee as long as the merchandising and sequel rights stayed with him. Fox agreed.

It was a historically bad call for the studio, but it is easy to see why they made it. Lucas was a relative newcomer to the Hollywood scene (AMERICAN GRAFFITI or not) wanting to make a space opera brimming with funny words like Jedi and Skywalker and a giant, talking dog. Lucas offered to take less money in exchange for some free words on paper. What would he do with merchandising rights anyway? Would he be able to license Kenner Toys?

Some believe that the reason Fox waived merchandising rights was simply that merchandising was not as developed as it is today. Fox had had a very difficult time trying to sell merchandise for its 1967 movie, DOCTOR DOLITTLE, and that gave Lucas an opening.

Fox was even less bullish on the potential for sequels. Fox did not view STAR WARS as a moneymaker, but as an $8 million handshake so that Lucas's next AMERICAN GRAFITTI would land on their doorstep. The chance of a way-out, sci-fi movie turning a profit was low, so they were dismissing sequel rights for a movie that would most likely never have a sequel.

After delays and special-effects issues, Fox would eventually increase the budget to $11 million which provided enough capital for Lucas to get the picture done. This is why THE EMPIRE STRIKES BACK and RETURN OF THE JEDI would become two of the biggest-budgeted, most-successful movies ever self-financed outside of the studio system.

Put yourself in Lucas's position at the time. He had achieved a great deal of success with AMERICAN GRAFFITI, but with a career path that had not yet been established. Nevertheless, he believed enough in himself and STAR WARS to turn down significant monies to retain such rights. He gambled large on STAR WARS and won big by retaining the merchandising and sequel rights just to reduce costs. He would be the only creator to ever establish a billion-dollar studio on the strength of a single motion picture ... and what would eventually become the greatest licensing programs of all time.

Over the past 40 years, STAR WARS became one of the top three most successful movie franchises in history and created a pop culture. The first film in the franchise, entitled STAR WARS, was released in 1977. It would generate two trilogies—a prequel trilogy and sequel trilogy. STAR WARS not only attained global notoriety but collected a ton of awards, being nominated for 29 Academy Awards and winning seven. The films were also awarded three Special Achievement Awards. Through 2020, the twelve STAR WARS movies grossed $10.3 billion worldwide and the ancillary products tripled that.

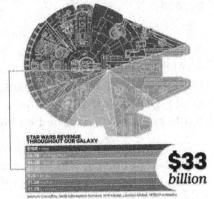

Disney bought Lucasfilm in 2012 for $4.06 billion, acquiring all merchandising rights as well as the distribution rights to all subsequent STAR WARS films, beginning with the release of THE FORCE AWAKENS in 2015. To date, the STAR WARS saga has produced nine live-action films with more in the works and has spawned an extensive media franchise including books, television series, video games, and comic books, resulting in significant development of the series' fictional universe.

Lucas combined a towering ego with his vision and an ability to play a finance game that set him apart from the typical Hollywood producer. "When I was writing," Lucas told *Rolling Stone* in 1980, "I had had visions of R2-D2 mugs and little windup robots, but I thought that would be the end of it. . . . All I knew was that I wanted to control the sequel rights because I wanted to make the other two movies."

From a licensing and merchandising perspective, one can find licensed STAR WARS products of literally all types and shapes in every retail venue in every country in the world, perhaps in the galaxy. And it all started as a world inside one man's head that almost no one else cared about.

ROCKY ... Its Gotta Be Me

ROCKY was a 1976 American sports drama film, written by and starring Sylvester Stallone. It was a rags to riches story of an unknown, uneducated, down-and-out fighter named Rocky Balboa who got a shot at the world heavyweight boxing championship. The original movie was a huge success, but the franchise it created was enormous.

When Stallone pitched his script in the mid-1970s, he was a Hollywood newcomer with no track record. Sylvester Stallone had a tough childhood—he was in an out of foster homes and unable to earn a steady income. He even had to sell his dog to help pay his electric bill.

Then his luck changed. Two weeks after selling his dog, Stallone sat down and wrote the screenplay for ROCKY in 3½ days after watching the championship match between Muhammad Ali and Chuck Wepner at the Richfield Coliseum in 1975. Wepner, who was the longest of long shots, was TKO'd in the 15th round of the match by Ali. While the fight may have motivated Stallone, he later denied that Wepner provided any inspiration for the script. Wepner would, however, subsequently sue Stallone, and the parties settled.

Stallone worked tirelessly to try to place it with a studio. After more than 1500 rejections, United Artists expressed interest and offered him $125,000 for the rights with one condition—they wanted someone other than Stallone to star in the movie, someone like Burt Reynolds, James Caan, or Ryan O'Neill. They were concerned that if Stallone was the lead, they couldn't attract a big-name director.

Negotiations continued. United Artists upped their offer to $325,000 with the same condition— no Stallone. Stallone remained firm. They finally compromised, allowing him to play the lead role if he agreed to accept $35,000 and a percentage of the profits of the movie as a concession. He agreed to proceed with the film, but not before buying back his dog.

The producers did have trouble casting other major characters in the story. Boxer Ken Norton turned down the role of Apollo Creed but would be replaced by Carl Weathers. Carrie Snodgress stepped aside from playing Adrian and was replaced by Talia Shire.

The film, made on a budget of just over $1 million with a further $100,000 spent on producers' fees and $4.2 million on advertising costs, became a sleeper

hit, earning more than $225 million at the global box office and became the highest-grossing film of 1976. It was nominated for ten Academy Awards, winning three, including Best Picture, Best Directing, and Best Film Editing. In 2006, the film was selected for preservation in the United States National Film Registry by the Library of Congress as being "culturally, historically or aesthetically significant". ROCKY is considered to be one of the greatest sports films ever made and was ranked as the second-best in the genre, after *Raging Bull*, by the American Film Institute in 2008.

Stallone recalls the experience saying that "it was insane" because at the time he was broke. Nevertheless, he believed in himself, held firm and the decision paid off. More importantly, the film solidified Stallone's career and set the path for his rise to prominence as a major movie star.

The film has spawned seven sequels: ROCKY II (1979), ROCKY III (1982), ROCKY IV (1985), ROCKY V (1990), ROCKY BALBOA (2006), CREED (2015), and CREED II (2018). The eight-picture franchise grossed over $1.5 billion on a worldwide basis. Stallone portrays ROCKY in all eight films, wrote seven of the eight films, and directed four of the six installments.

Stallone has also produced and starred in five RAMBO films which grossed more than $817 billion and three EXPENDABLES movies which grossed almost $800 billion worldwide.

In addition to box office success, ROCKY was a very successful licensing property. A paperback novelization was published by Ballantine Books in 1976 and several video games have also been made based on the film—the first for Coleco Vision in August 1983. Another was released in 1987 for the Sega Master System and in 1985, Dynamic Software released a boxing game for the Sinclair ZX Spectrum.

More recently, a *ROCKY* video game was released in 2002 for the Nintendo GameCube, Game Boy Advance, PlayStation 2, and Xbox, and a sequel, *ROCKY Legends*, was released in 2004 for the PlayStation 2 and Xbox. In 2007, a video game called *ROCKY Balboa* was released for PSP. In 2016, Tapinator released a mobile game named *ROCKY* for the iOS platform.

A musical written by Stephen Flaherty and Lynn Ahrens based on the film premiered in Hamburg, Germany in 2012 before moving to Broadway in 2014.

ROCKY licensed merchandise can be found everywhere, particularly in Philadelphia, although sadly, Stallone never received any portion of the revenues from the more than 100 licenses that had been signed as a result of the film. Those rights were retained by MGM.

You gotta believe in yourself!

V. Stories from the Road & Licensing Expo

Francesca Ash Reflects on Almost 40 Years of Licensing Expos

Whilst licensing activity carries on throughout every year, my overwhelming memories of years gone by in this industry are driven by some of the trade shows – and Licensing Expo in particular.

I am rather proud of the fact that I have only ever missed one show (1982 because I was heavily pregnant) and I was very much part of the very first show – at the Midtown Hilton in late May 1981. We had a little over 30 exhibitors and my highlight (or lowlight depending on which way you look at it) was being asked, at the last minute, to don the costume of one of the SEVEN DWARFS and march (if you can in a SLEEPY costume) down Sixth Avenue. If anybody reading this remembers the movie THE GRADUATE where Benjamin Braddock came out of his parent's house wearing a full sub-aqua suit and all he could see were his feet … well, that's how I felt on that hot Mayday!

That show was just the first of a series of shows that somehow each year sheds light on the growing and developing licensing industry.

Las Vegas Licensing Expo

Within a few years of the first show, the exhibition had become a little short of a jamboree. It seems as if anything, and everything, could be licensed – and very often was.

Just imagine three grown men, dressed as oversized raisins, promoting the California Raisin Association, and walking the aisles of the show, for the full three days with a boom box playing "I Heard It Through the Grapevine"!

There are a few "special" memories that stand out above all others.

One, without doubt, was CHARMING BILLY.

CHARMING BILLY was an angelic-looking six-year-old boy whose mother decided was licensable. The poor child sat, smiling, on a chair on their booth for three full days. Strangely enough, that was their first, and last, appearance at Licensing Expo.

Fast forward a couple of years later, and animals were the order of the day. The movie company MGM felt their booth needed "animating" and brought a full-sized, rather beautiful, lion who yawned his way through the three days of the show.

Another animal in the form of a chimpanzee wearing OSH KOSH dungarees and expertly weaving his way down the aisles on roller skates created interest for the lion who roared hungrily at the chimp every time he passed the MGM booth.

That same year there were cats, there were dogs (not altogether house-trained) and a plethora of other furry pets all of whom were looking for their big break. Again, strangely, they failed to materialize the following year.

My final, but somehow most entertaining, memory is the year when THE ATTACK OF THE KILLER TOMATOES was being revived and licensed. As expected, there was a large tomato costume. Sadly, it was so large that it was unable to go up or down the escalator at the Hilton without becoming wedged between the handrails. It took three people to help pull it off the escalator – whilst creating hilarity amongst the rather puzzled show visitors.

*****

Then, there was the story of signing in as an exhibitor at the Licensing Expo in Las Vegas. Upon my arrival at Mandalay after a long trip from London, I went to sign in and get my credentials. The very pleasant Advanstar person tasked with the responsibility of registering exhibitors started up a conversation with me, asking where I was from. When I told her, "London in the UK," she seemed a bit perplexed, inquiring, "did I fly or drive here?" That, of course, left me speechless.

The Blues Brothers Go to Vegas

SG Companies (also known as S. Goldberg) was a shoe and footwear manufacturer that was the first company to acquire a license for footwear. Back in the '50s, the company, under the leadership of Bernie Leifer, then the president of SG, licensed ROY ROGERS and the rest is history! In the good old days of licensing when licenses were cheap (and royalties were reasonable and we could make money) and success was a "real success", Bernie had the foresight to spot the winners — just to name a few, POUND PUPPIES, POKEMON, POWER RANGERS, TELETUBBIES, BRATZ, and many more.

Bernie recalls that while he was the chairman of LIMA, he came up with the idea of bringing the BLUES BROTHERS to the Licensing Expo. At the time, it was a very popular film starring Jim Belushi and Dan Aykroyd playing brothers Jake and Elwood Blues, who together make up an R&B band. As a spoof, Bernie and Charles Riotto dressed up as the BLUES BROTHERS and had an uncanny resemblance. The

50

video of them running through NYC jumping in a cab was shown to the licensing community at the Awards Ceremony. It was quite hysterical.

The best story I remember was when we were all celebrating at Mandalay Beach after the awards ceremony during Licensing Show. Bernie was hanging with his team and several others. Danny Simon came along to say hello to Bernie and the team which gave Bernie a challenge. Well, that is one thing you just don't do to Bernie because he will always come out on top and win. Suddenly, Bernie tackles and pins Danny in the sand. It was quite funny, and everyone enjoyed a good laugh.

Danny Simon's Ode to the Licensing Show

The year was 1990, the place, New York City's Javits Center, the time June, the event The International Licensing Show, the weather – miserable, hot and humid, with intermittent showers.

The Licensing Show has finally made to the big leagues – the Javits Center! Not a hotel ballroom, nor the now-defunct, dungeon-like Coliseum at Central Park, we are showing at New York City's main venue for conventions. Albeit the basement of the Javits Center, but what the hell. It was still the Javits Center.

As we begin the process of booth building, the friendly folks working there stopped by, perhaps to drop-off a welcome basket? Make sure that we didn't need anything? Nope to both, just a "friendly warning that you can't be doing what you're doing." That's someone else's job. Not born stupid, I quickly realized that I needed to draw upon the power of former Presidents. Two Jacksons cured the problem, and we labored on.

Didn't we order power for the booth? According to the form, there should be an outlet just over there. A hike over to the electricity stand and a chat with guys there confirmed that power was on the way. By the third same conversation, however, it became clear that a little incentive was required – this time a pair of Hamilton's.

As the show started to take shape, it became very noticeable that the room, one of the basement's four sections, might be just a bit too large. With a ceiling height that was a speck lower than the entrance to outer space and nothing in the room standing above 8 feet, with only three rows of booths, it was becoming evident that perhaps the room was a bit too large. By the end of the day, this observation was confirmed.

There we were. Three rows of hand-wrought booths running from the front to the back of the hall with ample space on either side of this rather voluminous room. In the confines of a hotel ballroom, the show seemed so much larger. With its very user-friendly three-row layout, a leisurely stroll, including a few stops to kibitz, about 30 minutes was ample time to cover the entire show. Here in this subterranean cavern, it was now clear that perhaps the planners had over-reached.

Today, with the Licensing Show's multi-level booths, intersecting lanes of letters and numbers and main isles sprinkled with couch-festooned rest areas, it is easy to forget the show's humble beginnings and the efforts of so many to build a world-class trade show.

Louise Q. Caron's Recollections from LIMA Gala's Past

Do You Know Who I Am?

Louise Q. Caron, former Sr. Vice President/Member Relations for LIMA, managed the Awards Gala for many years when it took place in New York City. She was always available at the door to greet the guests and troubleshoot any issues regarding tickets. Following are some recollections from her evenings as the "Gala Bouncer:"

- "Do you know who I am?" She can't tell you how many times she heard that one over the years!
- A man showed up without a ticket and said, "I don't need a ticket, I'm one of the founders of LIMA". When she asked him if he knew Murray Altchuler (LIMA's co-founder), he said, "Who's Murray?"
- Three people told her husband (who was helping me at the door) they were LIMA Board Members and didn't have their tickets. Her husband told them to, "See Lou." One of them asked, "Who's he?" Her husband responded, "You should know - SHE takes the minutes at every Board Meeting." They knew they were busted and headed back down the escalator.
- Two very friendly gentlemen told her they were from the United Nations and needed to meet their party inside. (They didn't have tickets, of course.) After a brief conversation, they hit the road. Even fake "diplomats" need a ticket!
- A gentleman told her he was a reporter with *The New York Times* and was there to cover the event. Even though LIMA did not give press passes, she asked him for credentials as she suspected he was not a reporter. He said he didn't carry ID. Nice try!
- "My Assistant has my ticket. She'll give it to you when she gets here." She didn't think so.

- A guy showed up saying he didn't need a ticket - he was a winner and was there to collect his trophy. She told him that was not possible as the winners are not announced in advance. He told her that he received a call from LIMA. Just to see what he would say, she asked him who called? He said, "some woman - I don't know her name". She responded, "that's not possible, only our President and I know who the winners are." By the way, he wasn't a winner.

- Next up: A man showed up without a ticket. She told him his name was not on the list and offered to sell him a ticket. He responded, saying that he didn't carry a wallet and had no cash, credit card, or ATM card to get cash. Who does that???

- An elderly gentleman showed up with his very young girlfriend without tickets. He was extremely indignant when he was told he could not attend as the event was sold out and he was not on the guest list. He then told her that he was invited to sit at a specific company table. She located a rep from the company and was told he had not been invited by them. When she relayed the response to him, he raised the cane he apparently needed to walk and pointed it just a couple of inches from Louise's face and yelled, "I'll have your job!" Okay, Dude – have a nice evening.

- "The Runners" - They are the folks that would occasionally make the mad dash and run right past her at the door. Louise's husband would head them off and bring them back to her. The runners never had a ticket.

- "The Bully" - The person who didn't have a ticket and had no intention of ever buying one. The bully would try to muscle his or her way in while speaking LOUDLY. One year, a man was particularly rude, not to mention relentless. He wouldn't take no for an answer and refused to pay. After a few minutes of loudly trying to intimidate her, he just stopped and left. Louise was happy that she had diplomatically handled the situation, not realizing that a moment before, her husband had appeared behind her and gave him "the look."

- Louise's personal favorite … A man wasn't able to get by her without a ticket, so he tried sneaking through a wall of tall plants. He didn't realize that the plants were hiding a stanchion and he fell into it and took a few plants with him. As he tried to crawl away, she asked him if he needed assistance. Really???

****

The Lion Sleeps Tonight

In the mid-1980s, the MGM lion was on exhibit at the show and a Shar-Pei dog named Major Ugly was also appearing at the show. The lion was napping when

Major Ugly came down the aisle for a walk. The lion woke up only to find Major Ugly relieving himself not far from his cage. He let out a roar and Major Ugly took off. This event made news when one of the exhibitors wrote a Letter to the Editor to one of the trade publications complaining about the show and how "animals were using the aisles as toilets." A bit of an exaggeration!

****

Early LIMA Award Winners—Like a Door Prize??

In the early years of LIMA, the awards process was quite different than it is today. There was no "call for entries" and there was not a specific group of awards

categories. Rather, the Board of Directors would develop a shortlist of unique properties, products, and agencies that would be recognized for their outstanding achievements in licensing during the past year. And, unlike today's program, the winners were announced in advance of the Awards Gala.

At the 1989 Annual Membership Meeting that kicked off Licensing Week, Murray Altchuler, LIMA's Executive Director, congratulated the winners that were going to be honored at the upcoming Awards Ceremony. After doing so, a hand went up. It was Seth Siegel, co-founder of Beanstalk and a future LIMA Board Member, asking, "How do you determine who gets an award? Is it like my daughter's birthday party? Anybody who walks in the door gets a prize?"

Seth's delivery was a pure matter of fact, no sarcasm, just looking to understand the process. It struck some as a funny observation of the Awards.

LIMA developed a shortlist of awards categories that members, as well as non-members, could enter the following year. Winners were selected by a vote of the membership and were not announced until the Awards Gala. A couple of years later, the categories were expanded and have evolved through the years to recognize the ever-changing licensing industry.

Some believe that it was Seth Siegel who started the discussion and set the wheels in motion for the LIMA Awards Program that exists today.

The Battle of Sixth Avenue

LIMA (now Licensing International) originally started as two separate associations back in the early 1980s: the Licensing Industry Association ("LIA") was formed for licensors and licensing agents and the Licensed Merchandisers' Association ("LMA") focused on licensees and manufacturers. Murray Altchuler, who was then a Vice-President at Licensing Corp. of America ("LCA"), became the LIA's first president, and Jerry Robinson, who ran Pilgrim Products, became the first president of the LMA. The two associations would ultimately merge in 1985 to form LIMA.

At the time, a group called Expocon headed by Fred Favata ran the annual Licensing Show which started in New York City in 1981. That show ultimately grew into what is now the Licensing Expo held in Las Vegas.

By 1983, both trade associations were rolling along, and they decided to stage their own shows in New York. Obviously, they never coordinated either the dates or venues of their respective shows because, as luck would have it, they were held at the same time in New York City at two different hotels on Sixth Avenue. If that wasn't confusing enough, the hotels they chose were both owned by Sheraton. Thus, there were two separate shows held across the street from each other, each in a Sheraton hotel. Thus, it was confusion, twice compounded.

Ultimately, the LIA show would move the following year to Atlantic City before closing and being folded into the Expocon show. Expocon and Advanstar ultimately bought out LIMA's rights in the show in 1997 but retained LIMA as its "Official Sponsor."

Steve Herman & Pizza to the Gala

Steve Herman, who would eventually head up licensing at, among other places, Archie Comics, Hearst, and Scholastic, recalls going to the Licensing Show in 1982 or 1983 and attending the Gala. He was sitting at a table of 10 listening to the interminable speeches as they continued to drone on and on. After literally hours, everyone was starving and starting to complain, somewhat noisily. At one point, Lester Borden, who ran  licensing at Columbia Pictures, excused himself to use the men's room. No one gave it a second thought until about 30 minutes later, a pizza delivery person approached his table with three steaming hot pizzas. Lester never admitted it, but everyone was treated to a slice or two of pizza as the speeches rambled on that day.

VI. Unique Licensed Products

Arlene Scanlan's Favorite Licensed Products

I have had a fair share of opportunities to develop *unique licensed products* in my career. Several that come to mind were a result of our initial representation of the Metropolitan Transportation Authority ("MTA"). We had been hired by the MTA to develop a traditional licensing program with certain criteria in mind. One was to license high-end products that would help elevate the brand, specifically moving away from licensing less than exemplar, touristy, novelty, and "tchotchke" products that had historically been the only items available to an institutional brand like the MTA. The second criterion was to work with licensees that made socially-conscious products and products that would help to reinforce the MTA's mission of sustainability. Most people do not realize that NYC was one of the cities with the smallest carbon footprint in the US. It is no surprise that this fact was in large part due to NYC's rapid transit system.

So, we set out to elevate the value of their brand and to look at sustainable products, wherever possible. So under "unique product," I would list the line of folding bikes we licensed, making it possible for people traveling throughout the city to easily bring their bike on the subway or bus with them. Next, we licensed a folding kayak. It was covered with the MTA map graphic and indeed folded down to a size that could fit into the trunk of a car and be carried like a backpack to bring to the Hudson River for a quick city row.

We then lined up some very high-end licenses including a gold and diamond collectible, limited-edition watch line from a company called Ball Watch, known exclusively for making timepieces that were developed when the only way to tell time had to do with the accuracy of the running of trains. Webb C. Ball was Chief Inspector for the train lines in 1891. His early inspection system was the beginning of the vast Ball network that would encompass 75% of the railroads throughout the country and cover at least 175,000 miles of railroad and, thus, was born the first accurate timepiece. Of course, we saw them as a perfect foe for the MTA. The watches commemorated the Grand Central Terminal Centennial and each watch was numbered and sold for between $3,000-$5,000.

We also worked with MONT BLANC on a $2600 limited edition leather backpack that was sold only in MONT BLANC stores. It was a black bag entirely and, to be honest when I received the sample, I could not figure out what about it made

it an MTA bag. I was instructed by MONT BLANC's attorney to open the small zippered compartment in the back of the bag and pull out a piece of waterproof fabric that was covered with the subway map and this could be used to cover the bag in the event of rain. AHA!

We also licensed a line of beautiful leather boots with TIMBERLAND. Each boot featured a different borough in NYC and had a different subway token hanging from the back.

During that same period, we licensed a talented artist to create unique, one of a kind, home products including chairs, tables, and trays, and even key chains using real MTA metal signs found in the subway system by the artist. I think that some of these are still in the Cooper Hewett Museum.

Examples of Unique Licensed Products

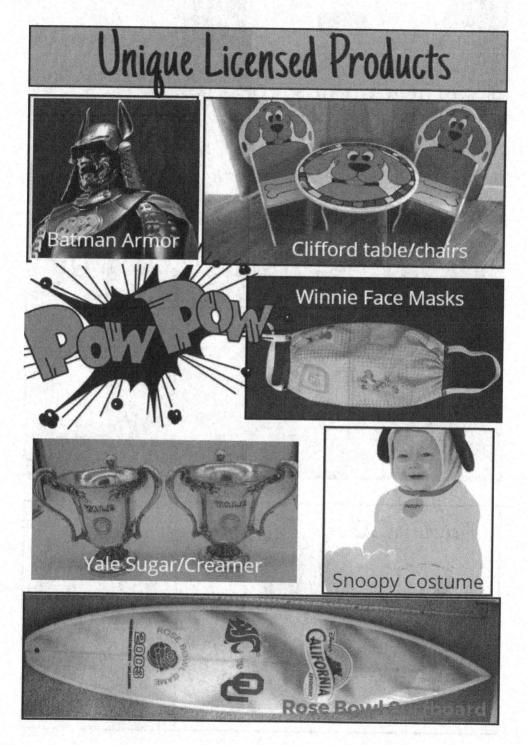

Notre Dame Jeweled Football

Packers Inflatable Chair

OREO ICE CREAM

GODFATHER WINE

Coca Cola Beverage Dispenser

Star Wars Statute

Lion King Coins

Ebbets Field Seats

Hershey's Cereal

LOONEY TUNES CHESS SET

M&M's Dispenser

LSU GAME TABLE

SUPERMAN PENDENT

Riverdale Pillow

Barbie Doll Furniture

WATERBABIES DOLL

Spiderman Dog Costume

WINNIE THE POOH POCKET WATCHES

VII. Auditing Trails

Mike Quackenbush's Memories

Henry VIII Look-Alike Licensee

My first ever licensing audit occurred in the summer of 1988 when I was a 3-year staff person at a regional accounting firm in Washington, DC. Our client owned valuable sports-related properties and wanted to conduct the first-ever audit of one of its licensees. I got the lucky assignment, or so I was told, of going to Dallas, TX in the middle of August.

Shortly thereafter I was on a plane to the licensee's office in Dallas to conduct an audit of their books and records. Upon arriving at the company, I was introduced to the licensee's president. I could not help but notice he was a complete look-alike for King Henry VIII. He even had a huge bowl of grapes in front of him on

his desk. For some reason, I always thought King Henry had eaten lots of grapes. In any event, King Henry got started by telling me about his company and then showing me a video of all the great things his company was doing. After the propaganda session ended, I began to audit their books and records and soon learned that King Henry had set up a dummy company to fraudulently create sales to lower the royalty paid to my client. I calculated that the licensee owed my client over $5 million. Upon notifying King Henry and his CFO of my findings, they went into immediate damage control. They made claims that were not true, stated that there was a side letter agreement and on and on. One of the odd things they asked me about was where I was staying that evening. Being a naïve twenty-something auditor, I told them the name of my hotel.

I finished up for the day at their offices and returned to my hotel to complete a little bit of work in my room. I ordered some room service and got to work. Later in the evening, there was a knock at my door. When I opened the door, I encountered a very attractive woman with a coat open to reveal what appeared to be a bathing suit and nothing else. Once again, I was a naïve twenty-something auditor, but I knew enough to know that the woman standing in front of me was not there to help me conduct the final audit steps of King Henry's books and records. It became more clear that the woman standing in front of me was probably employed in the world's oldest occupation when she said that she was sent by King Henry to provide as of yet unspecified services and asked me if she could come in. I politely declined and said that I was not interested but, thanks anyway.

I went back to King Henry's office the following day and he asked if I got the present that he had sent last night and could we review the audit results once more. At this moment I determined it was time to leave Texas and go home as the audit was taking a very unusual turn and I was concerned about what would be sent to my room that evening. I politely declined another meeting with King Henry and made a beeline for DFW and the first flight back to DC. Shortly thereafter, I generated my report on my findings for my client. About 6 months later, King Henry settled with my client for a multi-million-dollar payment.

****

Chinese Licensee's Multiple Set of Books

Then, there was the story of the corporate brand owner, headquartered in the United States, which retained us to conduct a worldwide licensing program. One of its licensees was a Taiwanese company that was operating in mainland China. In addition to selling licensed products, they were also operating a series of branded stores.

When the licensee's royalty payments appeared to be far below the level of activity, the property owner elected to audit the licensee's books which was their right under their license agreement. The licensee initially objected and, in typical fashion, was not cooperative in setting up a mutually convenient date. After some threats, the licensee finally consented and allowed us to review their books.

The actual review of the licensee's books turned out to be "challenging" at best, virtually "impossible" at worst. Every time our audit team visited the licensee's offices in mainland China, mysterious things happened which prevented us from completing the audit. On at least two separate occasions, the company experienced power outages at their offices which prevented the team from plugging in and powering its computers and, more importantly, made the task of reviewing computer books and records impossible.

Finally, the licensee and the audit team agreed to allow the auditors to have remote access to its financial records from the auditor's hotel rooms. After several stops and starts, the audit team was finally able to complete the audit, discovering, to their amazement as well as the amazement of the property owner, **that the licensee was maintaining** *four* **different sets of books documenting the transactions—4 sets of books???**

When this discovery was reported back to the property owner, the obvious question was why? We were asked if we had ever experienced any comparable situation. We indicated that we had, on occasion, come across a licensee who had two different sets of books, e.g., an actual one and a second set that may have been used for a government inspection or inspection by the licensor. We had never, however, seen any licensee maintain four sets of books, nor did we have any explanation for why they would do that.

The entire situation then led to a meeting between the licensee and the property owner and its counsel at which the licensee steadfastly maintained that they "had paid every penny that they owed the licensor," even though the audit report showed that the licensee was paying pennies on the dollar. Ultimately, the property owner decided to terminate the license agreement and move in a different direction rather than litigate against the licensee, considering the difficulties of litigating with a Chinese company in either the United States or China.

Charles Schnaid's Remembrances

Who Said You Can't Deduct Returns When Calculating Net Sales?

Many years ago, I was retained by legal counsel for a German licensee to provide services in an arbitration proceeding in New York between a US licensor and the licensee. At issue was the allegation that the licensee had not paid all the royalties due on the licensed product, a child's doll, due to its deducting unauthorized expenses relating to "returns" not covered by the agreement. It was an unusual license agreement in that royalties were based on gross sales, rather than net sales as is the typical case. The issue that surfaced, however, was whether the licensee was able to deduct returns in the context of gross sales. The provision in the agreement was not clear, since counsel for both the licensor and licensee had previously approved a change and had unintentionally omitted certain wording when preparing the final agreement. Both sets of attorneys had missed this.

The licensor's accountant, whose New York license had expired, had visited the licensee in Germany and had carried out minimum procedures before issuing a report which was incorrect and also mixed up the purpose of the report by confusing "audit" with agreed-upon procedures and consulting within his report. The licensee was able to show that they deducted what they understood to be legitimate deductions for returns of products from its customers. However, the arbitrator, who it seems had no or very little understanding of the issues relating to returns, ruled against the licensee.

This is a clear indication of how important the definition of deductions for royalty purposes, especially "returns", can be in the license agreement. Moreover, care should be taken in engaging experienced licensing attorneys and accountants as well as careful review of the Agreement before signature.

****

The POOH Wars

This was the largest and longest-running licensing case at that time (about 20 years ago). The case had been going on for about 12 years when I became involved.

Our firm was engaged by the Court for me to act as a neutral accounting referee. This was after about 20 accounting firms were interviewed in the offices of a large national law firm. Almost 30 thick files were delivered to me with instructions to familiarize myself with the contents and work in conjunction with a large national firm of accountants whom I would also supervise. We kept getting additional files as the court proceedings continued. It took a few years before the courts made their decision between the parties and neither I nor the accounting firm were called upon to issue any reports on our findings.

Millions of dollars were incurred in legal expenses by both parties.

****

Double Dealing by a Licensee

Several years ago, we were engaged by a major not-for-profit organization to audit one of their licensees. The license was for pet products. Despite our typical advice that our clients should "audit" their licensees sooner rather than later, this licensor waited about 4 years before proceeding.

Double-dealing: dishonest behavior and

actions intended to deceive.

Cambridge Dictionary

On visiting the licensee's facilities, we did our typical walkthrough to familiarize ourselves with the product and the licensee's operation. The product was equipment to allow dogs to exercise indoors by utilizing this apparatus. We noted that the licensee had essentially two lines of the same product—none of which were branded with our client's trademark. We also reviewed their advertising material, including ads that they had run in airline magazines displaying the equipment with complete details about the product and its benefits.

During our engagement, we soon found that the licensee was advertising the branded version of the licensed product. While they were advertising the branded products on which they were paying royalties, they were also selling the identical, unbranded version the sales of which were not being recorded for royalty purposes.

74

When we questioned the licensee, he denied that he intended to avoid royalty payments, stating that these products were developed by him and not subject to royalty payments although this unbranded line had the exact specifications and design as the branded line.

We communicated this to the licensor and computed the royalties owed, which came to a significant sum. The licensee did not have the funds to pay these unreported royalties and, after legal intervention, eventually filed for bankruptcy. Unfortunately, the licensor's delay in finally conducting the audit long after the commencement of the agreement, with no follow-up in the interim, enabled the licensee to spend the funds otherwise due to the licensor. A significant amount was lost and irrecoverable by the not-for-profit licensor.

The moral of this story? Audit early and often.

****

What Conflict of Interest?

After several meetings with a property owner's licensing manager of a public company, including proposals of different levels of service i.e., "audit", agreed-upon procedures, and consulting, we were engaged to "audit" their licensees' fashion products.

We communicated with the licensee requesting certain documents such as invoices in advance. However, they insisted that we first meet with their owner/CEO, accountant, and CPA. We agreed, and together with our client, attended the meeting. Before the commencement of the meeting, we had a walk through with the licensee to observe operations and inventory.

Thereafter, we had a full meeting discussing the audit provisions of their license agreement that had been in effect for several years. We also told them what documents we would require.

Shortly after returning to our office, we received a phone call from the licensing manager stating that the CEO's of both the licensor and licensee had  agreed that no audit was necessary. We were told that these parties were friends, trusted each other, and saw no need to audit the royalty transactions. We were very surprised, as was the manager but obviously, the licensee had used its influence to stop the procedures despite possible violations of the license agreement.

VIII. The League of Mutual Destruction

The BRATZ Wars

The newspaper headline which appeared at the end of this war read, "It's Finally Over: 8 Years of Mattel vs. BRATZ And No One's Getting Paid but The Lawyers." That probably best sums up the battle between Mattel and MGA Entertainment over the BRATZ property.

It all started in 2001 when MGA introduced the BRATZ doll called "The Girls with a Passion for Fashion!" which became an overnight success. MGA sold $97 million worth of BRATZ dolls in 2001 and a billion dollars' worth in 2003. Perhaps for the first time since BARBIE was introduced, Mattel felt threatened that it would lose its dominance in the doll market.

When Mattel learned that the man behind BRATZ was its former employee, Carter Bryant, it became incensed. In August 2000, while he was still employed by Mattel, Bryant had pitched his idea for the BRATZ line of dolls to two MGA employees. Bryant was called back to see MGA's CEO, Isaac Larian, and brought some preliminary sketches, as well as a crude dummy constructed out of a doll head from a Mattel bin, a BARBIE body, and Ken (BARBIE's ex) boots. The Zoe, Lupe, Hallidae, and Jade dolls in Bryant's drawings eventually made it to market as Cloe, Yasmin, Sasha, and Jade, the first generation of BRATZ dolls.

Bryant signed a consulting agreement with MGA on October 4, 2000, although it was dated September 18. Bryant gave Mattel two weeks' notice on October 4 and continued working there until October 19. During this period, Bryant was also working with MGA to develop BRATZ, even creating a preliminary BRATZ sculpt. A sculpt is a mannequin-like plastic doll body without skin coloring, face painting, hair, or clothing

MGA kept Bryant's involvement with the BRATZ project somewhat hush-hush, offering several explanations about its origin, e.g., it was developed by MGA's president and/or his children, by a focus group, etc. Mattel would, however, receive an anonymous letter suggesting that Bryant was the creator, and in 2004 this led to a lawsuit against Bryant in California state court. Bryant would counterclaim against Mattel and then remove the case to federal court where MGA joined the party.

The litigation would ultimately morph into multiple fronts involving multiple parties, even including MGA Mexico, alleging various causes of action, including trademark and copyright infringement, "serial copycatting," theft of trade secrets, state-based tort claims, and even RICO (Racketeer Influenced and Corrupt Organizations Act) claims. It also extended to actions between MGA and its insurance carriers alleging that the actions should be covered by MGA's insurance policies.

Some of the top law firms in the country got involved in the case. Mattel was represented throughout by the LA office of Quinn Emanuel, while MGA used several different firms, including Skadden Arps; Jones Day; O'Melveny & Myers; Christianson; Glaser; and finally Keller/Anderle. All these firms shared a common trait—high billing rates.

Discovery was beyond extensive. A review of the docket entries in the case indicated more than 800 individual docket entries, which is extraordinary. During the discovery phase of the initial trial, Mattel was granted the right to scan Bryant's computer for evidence and found pornography and software used to wipe hard drives. During the trial, the judge allowed Mattel's lawyers to introduce pornography as evidence, and to question him about it … not a normal occurrence.

On the eve of trial, Mattel settled with Bryant, leaving the two toy companies to continue the battle. At trial, Mattel argued that Bryant violated his employment agreement by going to MGA with his BRATZ idea instead of disclosing and assigning it to Mattel. Mattel claimed that it was the rightful owner of Bryant's preliminary sketches and sculpt, since Bryant had worked for them at the time. Mattel further claimed that MGA's subsequent BRATZ dolls infringed on Mattel's rights and that MGA had wrongfully acquired the ideas for the names "BRATZ" and "JADE," and, as such, the BRATZ trademarks should be transferred to Mattel.

Mattel won virtually every point in the District Court, with the jury finding MGA liable for infringing Mattel's copyrights. It awarded Mattel $10 million in damages which were about 1% of what Mattel had originally sought, because it found only a small portion of the BRATZ dolls were infringing. The court then did a very unusual thing and placed the BRATZ trademarks in a "constructive trust," enjoining MGA from selling certain BRATZ dolls.

The tide turned, however, in 2010 when the decision was appealed to the 9th Circuit Court of Appeals, which reversed the district court decision and remanded it back to the district court for a re-trial. In a decision entitled, "Who Owns BRATZ" written by then Chief Judge Alex Kosinski (who, seven years later, would prematurely retire after over a dozen former female law clerks and legal staffers accused him of sexual harassment and abusive practices), the Court found that multiple errors had been committed by the District Court. Finding that fashion dolls with a bratty look or attitude, or dolls sporting trendy clothing were unprotectable ideas, Kosinski concluded his decision, stating, "America thrives on competition; BARBIE, the all-American girl, will too."

On remand and retrial, the case turned, in large part, on the questioning by MGA's lawyer Jennifer Keller of the Mattel C.E.O., Robert Eckert, to wit:

> Q: Say I am eighteen, doodling away. I place my doodles in my parents' house in one of the drawers of my teen-age closet ... Twenty years later, I am hired by Mattel. I visit my parents' home and find doodles. Does Mattel own them?
>
> A: Yes. ... Probably, yes.

Some believe that this exchange turned the jury in MGA's favor because it not only found against Mattel but found in favor of MGA's countersuit for theft of trade secrets. They awarded $85 million in exemplary damages, $2,172,000 in reasonable attorneys' fees under its copyright claim, and $350,000 in costs.

The case went back to Chief Judge Kosinski who, once again, reversed the district court (in part), but this time more in Mattel's favor, vacating the exemplary damages award but allowing the $2M+ attorney's fee award under the Copyright Act. Kosinski editorialized at the end of his decision, stating: "While this may not be the last word on the subject, perhaps Mattel and MGA can take a lesson from their target demographic: Play nice."

Litigation between MGA and its insurance carriers continued as MGA sought to get their attorneys' fees covered and the carriers sought to recoup some of the fees that they advanced but fell under the fees that MGA was awarded.

MGA would later file an additional action in state court against Mattel in 2014 seeking $1 billion in damages.

So, at the end of the day, with essentially $0 damages being awarded, one can only wonder who were the real winners? It cannot be determined exactly how much the various law firms billed for their services, or were actually paid, but based on the numbers recited in some of the decisions involving MGA's insurance carriers, one could reasonably estimate that the total legal fees billed for both parties may have approached a half a billion dollars.

WINNIE THE POOH....and Disney Too

One of the most successful character properties of all time is WINNIE THE POOH, which has been commercialized for the past sixty years by the Walt Disney Company.

The property found its origin in a book by the British author, A.A. Milne, entitled *WINNIE-THE-POOH*, which was published in 1926. A sequel, entitled *THE HOUSE AT POOH CORNER*, was published in 1928. In 1930, Milne appointed Stephen

Slesinger as his licensing agent and, a couple of years later, Slesinger would assign his certain rights, including the merchandising rights, to Stephen Slesinger, Inc. ("SSI"). Slesinger died in 1953 but his wife, Shirley Slesinger Laswell, took over and did a phenomenal job of licensing POOH and his related characters, CHRISTOPHER ROBIN, PIGLET, EEYORE, KANGA, ROO, and TIGGER, for a variety of different licensed products.

In 1961, Walt Disney Productions entered into agreements with both Milne and SSI to acquire the rights to the POOH characters, intending to produce a host of entertainment products based on the property and further expand the licensing program. Under these agreements, Disney was obligated to pay SSI and Milne fees and royalties on all POOH products that it sold or licensed. Disney did just that as it expanded on the SSI licensing program. Its direct-to-retail license to Sears, Roebuck & Co. made POOH and the related characters household words.

Unfortunately, the relationship began to sour in the 1970s. In the early 1980s, SSI confronted Disney executives with a suitcase full of POOH stuffed animals, toys, and brochures for POOH promotions that they claimed they couldn't find on its royalty statements. After much negotiation, the parties entered into a new agreement in 1983 under which Disney reportedly paid SSI more than a million dollars in back royalties, and the parties agreed to adjust the royalty rate.

Peace was short-lived, however, as home video grew and POOH topped Billboard's "kid videos" list. While SSI expected their royalties to grow proportionally, they did not. That resulted in SSI filing a lawsuit against Disney in 1991, a lawsuit that would eventually become the longest-running suit in Los Angeles Municipal Court and would also morph into a series of federal court actions.

Billions of dollars were at stake. POOH videos, teddy bears, and other merchandise have generated billions of dollars for Disney—the same amount as MICKEY MOUSE, MINNIE MOUSE, DONALD DUCK, GOOFY, and PLUTO combined.

Both sides went through several lawyers but, at its height, a pair of celebrity lawyers faced off against one another. Disney retained Daniel Petrocelli, who had successfully represented the Goldman family against O.J. Simpson and defended Enron's CEO in a criminal trial. SSI turned to Bert Fields, who was best known for representing Disney's former chairman Jeffrey Katzenberg in a suit against Disney, as well as Michael Jackson and Harvey Weinstein.

The heavyweight battle resulted in the production of literally reams of documents and the taking of dozens of depositions and extensive motion practice. SSI maintained that Disney was stonewalling all requests for discovery while Disney argued that SSI was on a fishing expedition and was making voluminous document requests. The court appointed an accounting firm to audit Disney's books only to later dismiss the firm at Disney's urgings. Things became so contentious that a retired judge was appointed as a special master to oversee discovery.

While the parties slugged it out in litigation, Disney was aggressively expanding the number of its retail stores and licensed POOH products were flying off the shelves. It has been reported that SSI's annual royalties grew to more than $12 million.

SSI had Disney on the ropes when it was discovered that Disney had destroyed 40 boxes of files belonging to Disney executive Vince Jefferds, who had signed the 1983 agreement and who had since died. At issue were conflicting positions as to whether Jefferds had agreed to pay royalties to SSI on all video products, irrespective of what the agreement may have provided. SSI maintained that it had a contemporaneously prepared memorandum of such an agreement that vehemently disputed this position. Since Jefferds had died, his files were highly probative of the issue.

The judge was not impressed by Disney's explanation that the files were destroyed in the ordinary course of business and sanctioned Disney, finding that there was evidence suggesting these files had been "willfully" destroyed. As part of the sanction, he ruled that Disney would not be permitted to dispute SSI's version of the agreement, and the jury would be informed of Disney's actions. This ruling was appealed to and affirmed by the appellate court.

SSI had drawn first blood, and Bert Fields believed that that decision alone could potentially cost Disney billions of dollars.

The tide turned quickly, however, when it came out that SSI had committed discovery violations of its own—serious enough in Disney's mind to result in them moving the court to dismiss the action. It turned out that SSI had hired a private investigator who, over several years, obtained confidential documents from Disney's private offices, trash dumpsters, and the facility of a contracted document disposal company. Many documents of the documents bore "Confidential" and "Privileged" labels which would normally not be produced in the normal discovery process.

After a five-day evidentiary hearing, the trial court concluded that the private investigator had taken confidential documents from several locations and that SSI had, either explicitly or implicitly, authorized those activities and attempted to conceal them. Concluding that no lesser sanction could ensure a fair trial for Disney, the trial court dismissed the action.

SSI appealed, but the appellate court affirmed the lower court's decision, holding that the trial court could dismiss the action for misconduct if it concluded that no other remedy could ensure a fair trial.

While the terminating sanction resulted in the dismissal of the state court action, it did not end the dispute between the parties. SSI had brought an action in federal court alleging that Disney's use of the POOH characters had infringed their rights in the property and expanded that case to cover underpayment of royalties. After years of litigation, however, the federal district court also found in favor of Disney, holding that it appeared that the 1983 agreement had transferred rights in the POOH property to Disney and, as such, SSI could not claim that Disney's use of the POOH property was an infringing use.

SSI had also tried to extend the battleground to the Trademark Office, challenging Disney's trademark rights to the POOH characters in 12 different proceedings. They were eventually consolidated into a single proceeding by the Trademark Trial and Appeal Board which granted summary judgment in favor of Disney. That decision was affirmed on appeal.

Not to be left on the sidelines, Milne brought an action of its own against SSI in 2002 seeking to terminate the original grant of rights to SSI in 1931. That action was dismissed by the district court in 2005 considering the 1961 and 1983 agreements and was affirmed on appeal. The dispute over the award of attorneys' fees, however, continued through 2010.

This war lasted for more than 15 years, morphed into literally dozens of collateral litigations, and ran up legal fees that, no doubt, ran into the 8 or 9 figures. At the end of the day, however, the parties found themselves in essentially the same position they were when it all began. Thus, one must ask, who won?

IX. The Licensing Hall of Shame

WWE Smacks Down Its Licensing Agents

The SmackDown between the World Wrestling Entertainment's ("WWE") and its tag-team of former licensing agents, Jim Bell and Stanley Shenker, earned a spot in the Licensing Hall of Shame after a judge labeled Shenker a *"serial perjurer"* before fining and jailing these agents for a host of charges resulting from their collaboration in a million-dollar kickback scheme that they perpetrated.

The story began soon after Bell joined the WWE in the late 1990s as head of licensing. He reached out to and retained an old colleague, Stanley Shenker, and his company, Stanley Shenker & Associates ("SSA"), to help broker deals with licensees. Both individuals had extensive licensing experience before joining working for WWE.

Soon after Shenker got involved, the pair set up a Hong Kong company, called Stanfull Industrial Limited ("Stanfull"), which was used to divert royalty payments from such WWE licensees as Toy Island, Ringside and Jakks Pacific Inc. Over a four-year period between 1998 and 2002, Stanfull paid kickbacks to Bell of about $950,000, falsely designed as invoices for consulting services. This allowed Shenker to deduct such payments on his tax returns as purported business expenses.

When WWE became unhappy with its licensing program, it dismissed Bell and severed its relationship with Shenker. Instead of going away quietly and being satisfied with retaining its ill-gotten gains, Shenker commenced an action against the WWE in Connecticut state court for what he claimed were past due commissions. That action would ultimately bring the scheme to light, particularly after WWE began noticing certain irregularities in the licensing program. It would also lead to a second action, this time brought by WWE in federal court against Bell and Shenker and toy licensees, Jakks Pacific, Inc., and THQ, Inc.

The WWE had maintained as a defense in the state court action that Shenker conspired with Bell to defraud the WWE and its licensees of money, by: (1) improperly soliciting and splitting a series of kickbacks from at least one licensee, Trinity Products (Trinity); and, (2) improperly treating licensing transactions not otherwise commissionable to associates as if such deals had been procured and negotiated by associates, and subsequently splitting the commissions wrongfully obtained by associates as a result.

For well over two years, Shenker consistently and vehemently denied these allegations, testifying throughout the first three days of his deposition that: (1) every payment Shenker made to Bell was for "developmental projects" unrelated to the WWE; (2) these payments amounted to no more than $300,000 to $400,000; (3) associates received payments from Trinity according to a "separate oral consulting agreement" in which Bell was not involved; and (4) Shenker had no ownership interest in any companies other than associates, Creative Craft Company and a real estate venture co-owned with his daughter.

Apparently, unbeknownst to Shenker during the first three days of his deposition, the WWE had obtained copies of Bell Consulting invoices that had been inadvertently produced to the WWE which made clear the fact that Shenker had willfully perjured himself in deposition testimony and interrogatory answers. After being confronted with one of those invoices on the third day of his deposition, Shenker recanted much of his prior testimony, making more than 400 substantive changes to his deposition testimony, and admitting to having given deliberately false and misleading testimony. The recantations made clear that for months, Shenker had deliberately lied under oath.

PERJURY: deliberately gives false and misleading testimony under oath.

The WWE had also taken the deposition of the president of a WWE licensee, Trinity, who disclosed the scheme devised by Shenker under which Trinity would be granted an exclusive right to sell WWE licensed products to Wal-Mart if Trinity would pay Shenker a commission of 2% of those sales.

After hearing that testimony, Shenker also recanted his prior testimony denying such a scheme and finally admitted that: (1) he granted Trinity a secret exclusive right to sell WWE products to Wal-Mart in exchange for 2% of those sales; (2) he sought to conceal his agreement with Trinity from WWE's counsel; (3) Bell was a part of the arrangement; and,(4) it was not a mere "coincidence" that his company-issued checks to Bell were equal to exactly one-half of Trinity's payments to WWE, since Shenker had agreed to split those payments with Bell. Shenker also admitted that he had lied and deliberately misled the WWE regarding the Trinity arrangement.

Shenker admitted to a wide range of discovery abuses that included: (1) giving perjured deposition testimony; (2) providing perjured interrogatory answers; (3) fabricating evidence after instituting the present action; (4) facilitating the destruction of evidence after instituting the present action; (5) concealing evidence; and (6) conspiring with third parties to engage in other litigation misconduct.

These disclosures occurred after more than two years of extensive discovery, including four discovery extensions, the production of more than 92,000 pages of documents, the taking of more than twenty-five depositions, and the filing of more than 150 motions, briefs, and other pleadings.

The Connecticut state court judge did not take kindly to Shenker's conduct, labeling him a "serial perjurer", dismissing Shenker's action under a doctrine called terminating sanctions (remember the WINNIE THE POOH case), and referring the case to the U.S. Attorney's Office for prosecution.

Both Bell and Shenker pled guilty to a host of charges in 2005. Shenker was sentenced to 33 months in prison and three years of probation while Bell received an eight-month sentence and three years of probation. Shenker was ordered as part of his sentencing to pay $2.8 million in restitution to WWE. Bell was ordered to pay a $6,000 fine and more than $950,000 in restitution.

The Case of the Truncated Royalty Statements

A licensing consultant/manufacturer's representative had an agreement with a major licensee tasked with seeking out new licenses for the manufacturer. In exchange for his services, he was entitled to receive a small percentage of the royalties paid to the licensors. For example, if the manufacturer was paying its licensors a 12% royalty, the manufacturer was also obligated to pay the consultant an additional point or two. Thus, the consultant's commission was based on the royalties that the manufacturer was obligated to pay to the licensors secured by the consultant.

This is a common arrangement among licensing consultants. The underlying agreement in this case between the consultant and manufacturer provided that the consultant would receive this commission for so long as the client retained licenses with those licensors obtained by the consultant.

The consultant worked for the manufacturer for more than a decade, generating more than 35 licenses for the manufacturer. As is common in most consultant/agent agreements, the commission was to continue irrespective of whether the consulting agreement remained in force. The language of the agreement concerning post-termination compensation was clear, to wit:

> The Commission obligation shall continue for so long as you continue to sell, distribute or ship Licensed Products under license agreements or any renewal, modification, substitution or extension thereof . . . in all cases, you shall remain obligated to pay Consultant its Commission on Licensed Products sold under all such license agreements that are renewed or extended.

As the manufacturer built its business and continued its licensing activities with the licenses and licensees brought by the consultant, the manufacturer made a business decision that it no longer needed the licensing consultant and, as such, elected to terminate their relationship.

A dispute developed between the parties over the extent of post-termination compensation provision and the manufacturer decided, unilaterally, that it no longer needed to continue the commission stream post-termination, irrespective of the plain language of the agreement. The manufacturer refused to permit the consultant to audit its books and records as was the consultant's rights under the representation agreement.

When the parties reached an impasse, the consultant had no alternative but to initiate litigation against the manufacturer because it believed that literally hundreds of thousands of dollars were at stake. The case arose from the manufacturer's: 1) failure to pay commissions to the consultant that were due and owing; 2) a denial of the consultant's contractual right to audit the manufacturer's records; and 3) the manufacturer's failure to acknowledge manufacturer's obligation to pay the consultant any post-termination commission on all the license agreements brought to the manufacturer by the consultant that was entered into by the manufacturer during the term of the representation agreement and any extensions thereof.

The manufacturer played hardball in the litigation, refusing to provide the consultant with copies of the actual royalty statements provided by licensees that it had obtained for the manufacturer, despite a contractual requirement that it do so. That left the consultant with no alternative but to subpoena the royalty statements directly from the property owner/licensors to verify the level of its damages.

Surprise, Surprise! To the consultant's surprise, the actual royalty statements provided by the licensees differed markedly from the commission statements rendered to consultant by the manufacturer to support its original payment of a commission.

Surprise, surprise. To the consultant's surprise, the actual royalty statements provided by the licensees differed markedly from the commission statements rendered to the consultant by the manufacturer to support its original payment of a commission. The consultant "graciously" suggested that these differences were due to the manufacturer "truncating" or "rounding" the actual royalty payments.

A comparison between the actual royalty payments provided by the licensors and the copies provided by the manufacturer to the consultant showed, however, that the differences were far more than simple truncation. They were significantly understated for the clear purpose of underreporting the manufacturer's commission obligation.

The consultant's initial review of the first wave of these royalty statements from the licensors revealed a systemic under-reporting by the manufacturer of net sales to the consultant. For certain licenses in certain quarters, the manufacturer had underreported royalties by more than a million dollars, the result of which was a substantial underpayment of commissions to the consultant.

When these discrepancies in the first wave of actual royalty statements were brought to the attention of counsel for the manufacturer, with the knowledge that more actual royalty statements would be received in the future and the case would soon be converted to one for fraud, the manufacturer immediately sought to settle the action for a number that at least, arguably, made the consultant reasonably whole. Had the actual royalty statements not been received from the licensors, there would have been no way for the consultant to quantify the extent of the underreporting by the manufacturer and expose its fraudulent actions.

The lesson learned was straight from the Ronald Reagan playbook: "trust, but verify."

X. Neat Inventions and Inventors

TICKLE ME ELMO

The SESAME STREET-licensed "TICKLE ME ELMO" doll was one of the hottest selling dolls of all time. It was first released by Tyco Preschool in July 1996, with an initial supply of 400,000 units. The dolls sold well and remained widely available in stores until the day after Thanksgiving when they suddenly sold out. With the Christmas shopping season rapidly approaching, Tyco ordered 600,000 more dolls from their suppliers. The promotion of the product was helped by Rosie O'Donnell, who had shown the toy on her TV show in early October. This resulted in unexpected demand for the Elmo dolls, causing shortages in the stores that were carrying it.

The scarcity of the new toy resulted in a shopping frenzy with potential buyers, as availability became scarce. This resulted in buyers having to literally fight over the dolls and even getting injured in the process. A Walmart clerk was injured during a Midnight Madness sale when a crowd spotted him being handed a box of toys by another employee and charged down the aisle and trampled him. By the end of December, Tyco had sold a million units.

Across North America, shoppers and retail workers were reduced to their primal instincts to obtain this must-have toy of the holiday season. The TICKLE ME ELMO doll combined the appeal of the popular SESAME STREET character with a novel design that allowed him to be "tickled" until he was practically out of breath.

Tyco's then-president, Neil Friedman, recalled years later that, "When you played with TICKLE ME ELMO for the first time, it brought a smile to everyone's face. It was a magical surprise."

While the marketing aspects associated with the product were a story onto itself and led to several B-School lectures on how limited availability of a product can increase sales, the actual development of the product was, perhaps, even more interesting.

TICKLE ME ELMO started with a concept called "TICKLES THE CHIMP" which had been created by two toy-industry veterans, Greg Hyman and Ron Dubren. Legend has it that Dubren had been walking in the park one day and saw a bunch of kids tickling each other. That brought back memories of his childhood and how much he loved tickling and being tickled. The pair then thought it would make a good toy. Unfortunately, their initial presentations of the concept to a dozen or so other toy companies were unsuccessful ... not uncommon for toy inventors.

Fortunately, however, technology caught up and the incorporation of sound chips in toys became cost-effective and, therefore, popular. The incorporation of sound in toys started with the TEDDY RUXPIN doll which had incorporated a cassette recorder in its torso. While effective, it was expensive. The development of less expensive sound chips followed which opened the door for their use in the TICKLE ME products.

The inventors worked to develop a doll or figure that it would laugh when you tickled it once; laugh harder when you tickled it again; and, finally, laugh hysterically when you tickled it for the third time. According to Dubren, the escalation was important since there was a beginning, a middle, and an end.

Having gone back to the drawing board with a revised chip, the inventors renewed their efforts to license the concept, again unsuccessfully. Enter Stan Clutton, who was the inventor liaison at Tyco and who was at least willing to listen to Dubren's ideas. Unfortunately, Clutton had a reputation for saying "no" more often than "yes" or even "maybe," which, again, was not unusual in the toy industry.

In a rare, some may even say "out of character" move, Clutton finally said "yes" to a prototype of TICKLES THE CHIMP. Clutton did say, however, that "this would be great as an ELMO doll, but we don't have the rights."

Unfortunately, Tyco did not have the rights at the time to the SESAME WORKSHOP characters—those rights had been licensed to Hasbro. Tyco did, however, have the plush rights for the LOONEY TUNES properties so they explored adapting TICKLES THE CHIMP to a TICKLE ME TAZ (for TASMANIAN DEVIL) and also explored TICKLE ME versions of BABY BUGS BUNNY and TWEETY.

Things changed quickly. Tyco would soon lose the rights to the LOONEY TUNES characters and replace them with licenses for the SESAME STREET characters, including ELMO. Hence, TICKLE ME ELMO became a possibility.

Gene Murtha recalled, "In those days, Tyco had no email system. We all communicated via fax. I remember being at the offices in New York after hours—it was me, Stan, and a few others. I walked past the fax machine and it was spitting out a notice that Tyco had dissolved their agreement with Warner Bros. I walked to Stan and said, "Why don't you take this and make TICKLE ME BIG BIRD?" And he said, "No, it would be TICKLE ME ELMO." Elmo's Law (coined by Dubren) came into effect, i.e., "anything that can go right, will go right."

Clutton's decision to go with ELMO was not the no-brainer that it appeared in retrospect. At the time, the SESAME STREET properties were more associated with educational products than mass marketed toy products, and the educational market was often considered a graveyard for mass-market toy products. This concerned Dubren.

Work continued on the product, and it was determined to add a laugh and shake feature, like the old-style flip phone that vibrated and shook as it was ringing. One concern, however, was that parents might think that the doll was having a seizure rather than simply shaking from laughter. This concern proved unfounded, however, after playtesting.

Perhaps the biggest innovation to the product was the incorporation of a "Try Me" feature so that the consumer could see what the product would do while on the retail shelf. It would immediately catch the buyer's attention in a matter of seconds as they were walking down the aisle of the store. This required including batteries in the packaging, a potential problem since the batteries could wear out before the customer took the product home. Neil Friedman, who had just joined Tyco, believed that such a feature was essential to convince the consumer to see the product before purchasing it and championed the idea.

TICKLE ME ELMO got the most attention during the New York Toy Fair in February 1996. The Today Show's Al Roker saw it and loved it and the Today Show's anchors spread the word far and wide.

An appearance by Neil Friedman on the Rosie O'Donnell show help create public interest. While Friedman was good, ELMO was great in pitching the product. Tyco had forecasted 100,000 pieces in September but after the Rosie show, the forecast increased to a million. Increasing a forecasted product tenfold brought a whole new set of problems—mostly on the supply side. Increasing the supply of the components was far easier than increasing the mechanical components. Tyco found itself building new tools virtually every week.

The supply problems translated into delivery problems, resulting in a scarcity of products at retail. This created a consumer frenzy as buyers were scrambling to obtain the few available units. TICKLE ME ELMO turned into the most coveted holiday item on wish lists everywhere, and the scarcity of products was hyped by the media causing even more consumer demand. John Gotti, Jr., son of late Mafia boss John Gotti, was seen entering a Toys "R" Us after hours and walking away with several Elmo's; Cartier Jewelers offered Elmo free with the purchase of a $1 million necklace. One Toys "R" Us manager watched in horror and cried as parents tore into them without regard for anyone's safety.

Business School marketing professors called the roll-out genius on the part of Tyco, but the reality was that it was not planned or, for that matter, welcomed. Managing inventory against proposed sales is critical since a toy company never wants to be stuck with inventory. Ultimately, Tyco would first transport units by ship but as supplies dwindled and demand exploded, it was forced to bring more by air, at far greater expense.

By the time Christmas came, it was clear that not everyone who wanted an Elmo was going to get one. That led to a slew of requests by the elite in both Hollywood, television, and sports who were willing to trade favors for a unit or two. It gave Tyco leverage with retailers who, heretofore, had been slow to pay invoices, but were now paying on time.

If that was not complicated enough, this all occurred while Mattel was in the process of buying Tyco and merging Tyco Preschool into Fisher-Price. It is believed that the entire purchase price of the acquisition of more than $700 million was funded by two-year sales of the ELMO products. By the end of 1996, TICKLE ME ELMO established itself as one of the most popular toys of the 20th century with over 1.2 million units sold in 1996 and an additional 4 million in 1997.

Tyco and Mattel were not the only beneficiaries of the ELMO success. The product launch and ultimate product line put SESAME WORKSHOP on the map as a major property owner and licensor for the mass market. SESAME WORKSHOP founder Joan Ganz Cooney acknowledged that the huge success of TICKLE ME ELMO allowed it to expand internationally.

POUND PUPPIES

POUND PUPPIES was a popular toy line introduced in 1984 and would later inspire an animated TV special, two animated TV series, and a feature film. Since its

introduction, POUND PUPPIES have generated over $1 billion of retail sales. POUND PUPPIES and POUND PURRIES sold over 200 million units worldwide.

The POUND PUPPIES property was created by Mike Bowling who, at the time, was an 18-year Ford assembly line employee. The pay was good, he had seniority and medical benefits but, unfortunately, he disliked his job. While driving with his young daughter, he became fascinated at how attached she was to her doll. She took it everywhere. To her, it was real. Bowling began thinking about the strength of that attachment, comparing it to that of a person and pet and the idea for POUND PUPPIES was born.

There were plenty of plush dogs in the marketplace at the time. What he did with POUND PUPPIES was to create their own identity within the category. Marketing and the name were what it was all about. They were POUND PUPPIES, so they came from a specific place! They did not have an identity, though, until the child picked it out, brought it home, and then determined the pet's sex, name, and personality, usually mirroring their personalities.

Even if you had two identical white, long-eared POUND PUPPIES on the shelf, a boy could come up and pick it and call it Spike, and a girl could pick it and call it

Susie. Other companies wanted to create breed-specific dogs and give them a name. Bowling felt that you could not do that and succeed.

Bowling had no money, no experience, and no directional map to success. He hired a patent attorney and toy consultant. "You can't sell an idea," Bowling said, "but you can sell a patent, a copyright, and a trademark."

He found craftspeople to create a professional prototype based on a floppy-eared stuffed dog. Its design featured forlorn, expressive eyes and promoted holding and hugging the puppy. (Loveable! Huggable!) Bowling created original handmade POUND PUPPIES which he sold to fellow workers at the Ford plant. He signed them and told his fellow workers they would be worth a lot someday when POUND PUPPIES became a huge success.

Even with a professionally crafted toy with packaging that looked like a dog carrier from the pound, the idea was rejected by 14 toy companies. Most of the toy companies that turned Bowling down did so strictly as a marketing decision. They were not looking for a plush toy that year. They might have already had a plush toy they were ready to introduce.

Mike's favorite story of rejection was when he presented POUND PUPPIES to the president of Ideal Toys at their offices in New York City. Bob Steiner, Mike's agent consultant, arranged the presentation, stating he had given the gentleman they were meeting his first job in the toy industry. Subsequently, the man shot up quickly as a star in the industry, becoming president of Ideal Toy. So, because of Bob Steiner's relationship, he told Mike, "We have a great "in" for this presentation!"

Mike shares it this way, "We had a one-on-one presentation in the Ideal conference room. Once the presentation was over, he looked at me and said, "That's the ugliest thing I've ever seen ... it looks like its squatting to pee!" Then he said he had a meeting to go to and walked out! I looked at Bob and said, "I am sure glad you had an 'in' with this guy!!"

Bowling was persistent and determined from the start to succeed, even if he had to make some handmade toys himself and build them slowly to become a craze. He knew about the CABBAGE PATCH success which was a craze before it hit the toy market. It was slow-rolling and kept going and going. Had all the toy companies turned him down, Mike said, "I would have made my own and built it that way."

Irwin Toys from Canada were the first to say yes and acquired the licensing rights in 1984.

Bowling said he never worried about being able to make a living. While employed at Ford, he collected his weekly paycheck plus benefits. Very few people are willing to pursue their ideas and dreams because they are reluctant to risk losing their comfort and security for a dream that could fail. But Bowling had the courage of his convictions and truly believed in himself. What makes this story particularly interesting and his choice even more poignant is that at the time Bowling had a child with cerebral palsy. Leaving Ford with decent pay, a health insurance program, and other strong benefits to journey out on his own with POUND PUPPIES could not have been an easy decision. Trading security for something as risky as launching a new toy product was difficult, but Bowling saw POUND PUPPIES as an opportunity to succeed, get out of the factory, and be able to take care of his daughter in any way, shape, or form. It has proven to be true.

After it finally reached the marketplace, Bowling recalls that he went to Canada for a business meeting. On his return, while waiting at the airport, he found himself sitting across from a little girl with a POUND PUPPY—the first one he had ever seen in the marketplace. He said that he sat quietly watching her hug on it and beamed, knowing that his struggle to take his idea to market was truly worthwhile.

Things exploded in 1985 when Tonka, wanting to expand its brand past toy trucks, licensed the U.S. rights. By that time, Bowling was $85,000 in debt. With the $100,000 advance from Tonka, one of the greatest joys of his new career was depositing that first check and paying back every one of his creditors. In 1985, Tonka sold more than 2.5 million puppies, leading to an animated TV series based on the characters. POUND PUPPIES made Time magazine's "All-Time 100 Greatest Toys"

list. One of the unique features of the property was that it was the first truly unisex toy. Bowling said girls make up 60% of the sales and boys the other 40%.

POUND PUPPIES was a hot promotional property. In 1987, in four weeks before Christmas, Hardee's restaurants offered a series of four different POUND PUPPIES to purchase with their children's meals. They did this promotion for two years and sold 28 million in a total of eight weeks! This was followed up with other successful promotions with Pizza Hut, Dairy Queen, and Long John Silver's.

A TV special based on the toy line was released in October 1985 by Hanna-Barbera which ran in syndication, and a videotape line was released in 1986 by Family Home Entertainment. A POUND PUPPIES television series was broadcast on ABC from 1986 until 1989. A second television series produced by Hasbro Studios premiered on the Hub Network (now Discovery Family) in 2010.

In 1988, TriStar Pictures released a POUND PUPPIES movie entitled *POUND PUPPIES and the Legend of Big Paw*.

The POUND PUPPIES toy line continued to be popular through 2002 when it was discontinued, only to be revived in 2014 by Funrise. In 2019, a new line of POUND PUPPIES was introduced by Basic Fun which went back to their original design. They have proven once again to be a big hit!

94

One of the biggest rewards for Bowling is the many, many, many stories he has heard throughout the years involving POUND PUPPIES. People love sharing their personal stories of how POUND PUPPIES were such an important part of their childhood. One man told him that he was driving his family home from a vacation out west when his daughter realized she had forgotten her POUND PUPPY at the last hotel they had stayed in. The daughter said, "You have to go back and get my POUND PUPPY!" He offered to buy her a new one, but she said, "No! You can't leave my POUND PUPPY behind!" So, he had to turn around and drive two hours back to the hotel to retrieve her POUND PUPPY. That is how much it meant to her!

TRIVIAL PURSUIT

According to *Time Magazine*, the board game TRIVIAL PURSUIT is "the biggest phenomenon in game history" in which winning is determined by a player's ability to answer general knowledge and popular culture questions. Players move their pieces around a board with the squares that they land on determining the subject of a question they are asked from a card. Categories included "history," "science and nature," etc. Each correct answer earns a plastic wedge that is slotted into the answerer's playing piece.

The game was conceived in 1979 by Chris Haney, a photo editor at the *Montreal Gazette*, and Scott Abbott, a sports journalist for the *Canadian Press*. Haney had originally dropped out of school at the age of 17 to take a copy job with the *Canadian Press*, the company his dad worked for. Haney would later state that

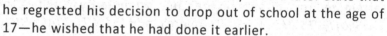

he regretted his decision to drop out of school at the age of 17—he wished that he had done it earlier.

The pair conceived the game while playing a game of SCRABBLE after it turned out that a couple of pieces were missing. While conceived in 1979, it took two more years for the pair to complete and commercialize the game in Canada.

Before doing so, however, they first needed to learn about the industry. To do that, the pair attended the Montreal Toy Fair, pretending to be a reporter and photographer doing a story on board games. They interviewed game makers on various aspects of board game development and said later that they got "$10,000 worth of information."

Armed with what they thought was a good concept and at least a fundamental knowledge of the industry, they realized that they needed money. They ultimately found 32 small investors, including Haney's brother, raising a total of about $40,000. It would have been 33 investors, but Haney convinced his mother not to invest because he was not sure it would succeed. They found a teenage artist, Michael Wurstlin, to create the artwork for the game in exchange for a small share in the company that they would ultimately form.

On November 10, 1981, the TRIVIAL PURSUIT name was registered as a trademark. That same month that they distributed 1,100 copies of the game in Canada. The first copies of TRIVIAL PURSUIT were sold at a loss—their $75 per unit manufacturing costs were 5 times higher than their $15 retail selling price.

The game took off in Canada, so much so that Selchow and Righter, a major U.S. game manufacturer and distributor, licensed the rights in 1983. Using an aggressive public relations effort, TRIVIAL PURSUIT became a huge success in 1984, selling a record 20 million games in the United States with retail sales reaching nearly $800 million.

The rights to the game were licensed to Parker Brothers in 1988 after initially being turned down by the Virgin Group. Hasbro acquired the rights in 2008 for $80 million. Reportedly, the original 32 investors have stated that they have been able to live comfortably on the royalties they have received for the rest of their lives.

In December 1993, TRIVIAL PURSUIT was named to the "Games Hall of Fame" by *Games Magazine*. By 2014, more than 50 special editions of TRIVIAL PURSUIT had been released. Players can test their knowledge on everything from LORD OF THE RINGS to Country Music.

More than 100 million games have been sold in at least 26 countries and 17 languages with estimated sales of $2 billion. Numerous editions of the game have been put out in various mediums, and several different television shows have attempted to capitalize on the game's popularity including three in the U.S., *TRIVIAL PURSUIT*, *TRIVIAL PURSUIT: America* and *ESPN TRIVIAL PURSUIT*.

The game has been the subject of several litigations. In October 1984, Fred Worth, author of *The Trivia Encyclopedia*, filed a $300 million lawsuit against the distributors of *TRIVIAL PURSUIT,* claiming that more than a quarter of the questions in the game's Genus Edition had been taken from his books. The district court judge disagreed, ruling in favor of the *TRIVIAL PURSUIT* inventors. The decision was affirmed on appeal.

A second suit was raised by a person who claimed that he invented the game and explained it to Haney. The litigation dragged on for years, but ultimately Haney and Abbott prevailed.

WATERBABIES®

One of the most endearing stories of the toy industry was the WATERBABIES doll story, created by Dan Lauer and licensed to Playmates Toys in the late 1980s.

The doll was inspired by Lauer's childhood memory from the 1960s when he and his sisters would fill up two balloons with warm water and draw a face on one of them to make warm, jiggly babes which they would wrap in a diaper. The WATERBABIES doll ultimately became the number one promotional doll in America when it was licensed to Playmates Toys in 1991.

At the time Dan came up with the idea and decided to try to license it, he was working as a vice president of Royal Banks of Missouri and decided to pursue a seemingly absurd passion – creating baby dolls. He liked the warmth and weight of the water dolls and worked to find a way to bring them to market.

He first began imagining WATERBABIES in January 1988, relying on what he called "pure possibility," i.e., believing that he could do anything that he wanted to do if he worked hard enough. He went the traditional route of trying to convince toy companies that they should carry his product. His first prototype was a balloon and 4 condoms. After many months and 700 rejection letters, however, he decided that he needed to turn his dream into reality and take the product to market by himself, or at least with a group of friends and family investors. He noted that the rejection letters indicated that they liked the "why" but questioned the "how."

So, he decided to quit his job with the bank and concentrate on taking the product to market. Friends and family did not universally agree with that decision. His mother cried and tried to convince him out of it. Even his in-laws counseled against it—advising him to stay with the bank job and do it on the side. They passed up an opportunity to invest in the doll.

He raised enough capital to get his idea off the ground and onto store shelves, raising about $500,000 and producing about 5,000 dolls. Store buyers agreed to carry the product and gave him enough affirmation to take the next step to begin making the dolls. Unfortunately, however, everything went wrong. On its first shipment to market, 7 out of 10 products failed. They leaked. He went back to his "world headquarters," i.e., his apartment, and consulted with his advisors— friends and family. They took the untested products, put them in a bathtub, and started checking for leaks. They glued the ones that were leaking and carefully put them back in the box in such a way that they did not look damaged.

Next, Dan needed to get the word out about his product. He had marketing monies in place, about $30K, but typical commercials at the time cost about $300,000. One of his early customers noted that the product was essentially a warm and cuddly hot water bottle and it was cold outside. He suggested that Dan stand in front of the store with attractive women and hand them to customers. Dan said, "thank you!" They sold hundreds of units an hour.

They then started sending a truck every night to the factory in the Bronx. The local test market ended with over 15,000 dolls sold instead of 5,000. Suddenly they had orders for 60,000. That was their "tipping point."

That led to the product being picked up by some of the major toy store chains with the potential of hundreds of thousands of new orders. Dan recognized that it would be difficult, if not impossible, to fulfill these orders. Fortunately, the toy stores' excitement caught the attention of some major toy companies who liked the product and, perhaps more importantly, saw the potential for significant sales. This led to what became a "bidding war" for the right to the doll from at least five of the major toy companies.

The winner of that bidding war was Playmates Toys headed up by Richard Sallis. Playmates Toys started as a Hong Kong-based toy company but eventually opened a California office. Playmates had generated more than $500 million in sales the prior year and were the first toy company in history to generate over $200 million in pre-tax profits, mostly on the strength of a license for TEENAGE MUTANT NINJA TURTLES which had become a top-rated Saturday morning cartoon show and the first motion picture which grossed more than $200 million worldwide.

Playmates introduced the WATERBABIES doll which almost immediately became the number one selling promotional doll in America and the second best-selling large doll of all time behind Cabbage Patch Kids.

With 27 years of a continuous distribution, more than 24 million WATERBABIES dolls have been sold around the world. The rights to the doll would eventually pass to other toy companies, and it is currently marketed by Just Play Toys. WATERBABIES' best days may be ahead. In 2021 WATER BABIES LOVES CLEAN WATER will make its debut teaming with water charities to help end the water crisis. As for Dan Lauer, he is currently the Founding Executive Director of USML Accelerate at the University of Missouri St. Louis, whose mission is to catalyze developing students, faculty, and the community to inspire entrepreneurship and innovation.

XI. Celebrity Jeopardy

Athletes & Beer Commercials

This comes from an interview with Marty Blackman in the *Merchandising Reporter* in April 1983:

MR: What are some of the more noteworthy instances of your involvement in connection with the use of sports personalities or teams in advertising?

BLACKMAN: Probably the most famous is the LITE BEER commercial from the Miller campaign. That instance did not involve the use of active players. Instead, retired professional athletes were used because of a Federal Alcohol, Tobacco and Firearms regulation that prohibited the use of active athletes who many children see as heroes, in advertising for alcohol and cigarettes.

MR: How about somebody like Billy Martin? How were you able to use him? He is still active in baseball.

BLACKMAN: He's a manager, not a player. The prohibition goes to active professional athletes only. It does not go to managers. Now each league has

different rules and regulations on this subject. For instance, I tried to get John Madden to do a MILLER commercial for over 2-3 years before he finally did one. But in his coaching contract, like all NFL coaching contracts, was a prohibition against any involvement with alcohol. He could not do it because of league rules. It had nothing to do with the federal government. The federal government would say, "Madden, you want to do it, you can do it, you're a coach", but the league coaching contract said no. Now, whether that would stand up legally or not is another question.

MR: Do any other leagues have funny rules like that, different than what you would expect?

BLACKMAN: That's about the most glaring. Baseball allows their managers to do it, football tries to prevent it.

MR: Do you know if any problems were encountered with the American Express commercial where Tom Landry and four individuals dressed in Washington Redskin uniforms (I assume not actual players) walk into a bar?

BLACKMAN: Probably not, because that was set up as a tough cowboy stereotype, opening swinging doors and walking into the bar. It is close though. You do not see them with beers in their hands or anything like that. But it is a good question, why the league should not have objected.

****

Mean Joe Greene Commercial for Coca-Cola

This comes from the same interview with Marty Blackman in *the Merchandising Reporter* in April 1983:

MR: Take the Mean Joe Greene example, did you first approach NFL Properties?

BLACKMAN: You do not need to do it simply to use Joe Greene. All you need is Joe Greene's permission and the NFL team must not object. That objection cannot be unreasonable. If they have an objection, it must be based on certain grounds.

MR: What can those grounds be?

BLACKMAN: That the campaign relates to an alcoholic beverage, that it relates to a product that reflects badly on the sport/team, for example, if Joe Greene was asked to endorse a Las Vegas casino. They would have the right to step in and object but, barring that, it is not easy for a team to object, although sometimes they will when it is in direct competition to their sponsors. Now when I say object, I do not mean that they will refuse the guy, it's just that they will try to dissuade him. For instance, using the Greene example, let's assume SEVEN-UP was tied in heavily to the Pittsburgh stadium or the PITTSBURGH STEELERS, e.g., they had run SEVEN-UP kids' day there, etc. In other words, they were the central soft drink in the Pittsburgh Steelers potpourri of promotions. In that situation, you might get the team saying to a player, "Hey look,  you're working for our sponsor's biggest competitor. You know SEVEN-UP gives us the scoreboard, you know they run clinics for kids, you know they advertise on Chuck Noll's pre-game show, etc. — and now you want to work with COKE? Hey, please, don't do it." The STEELERS, by the way, are the wrong team to use, I am just using this as an example. I would never think that the Rooney's would ever stop a guy from doing anything. I am using it only as an example.

MR: Does it make a difference if Joe Greene is wearing his STEELERS uniform or not?

BLACKMAN: Yes. If he is to wear the uniform, you must go and get a license from NFL Properties. NFL sells licenses based on the territory you are asking for and scope of use, e.g., the number of commercials, the commercial length, etc. A price is negotiated based on those set of facts. If you want six teams, (let's assume you are doing your thing along the eastern seaboard) that's going to be a different price than just one team. What we got for COKE and negotiated with NFL properties was the right to use the uniform in a one-time television commercial. When you want to use exact uniforms and logos, perhaps the team facilities, you are in a straight licensing situation with NFL Properties. If you are satisfied with other than official uniforms and can do without using official logos, then you do not need a license. You must have seen this type of ad many times, where a guy is dressed in a generic uniform or a sweatsuit. In those cases, you do not have to go through licensing with the league or the teams, but it is a very touchy area. The NFL is probably the most aggressive in protecting their rights. They'll even question you if you use a sweatshirt that has "Dallas" on it with the claim that when you have "Dallas" on a sweatshirt with the blue and silver colors, it means only one thing, the DALLAS COWBOYS. I am not saying they are right or wrong, but they are very protective of it. I don't think that the NBA would go after you or anything like that if you had a shirt with "Boston" on it. I am not saying the NFL would prevail, but they are extremely aggressive in attempting to protect their licensing trademarks and logos and anything that resembles their teams' writing script. So, you always must be aware of whether the commercial or promotion requires an NFL license.

Nell Roney on How SPUDS McKenzie Went from Fame to Shame

How SPUDS MACKENZIE, The Original Party Animal for BUD LIGHT, went from fame to shame in two short years. And it was not even his fault!

Another animal brand spokesperson—what could go wrong? Aren't animals easier to work with and less risky than human celebrities? After all, animals can't talk, can't be sued for sexual harassment, or accused of something even worse, right?

In the late '80s, a new, rather unexpected, and entertaining brand spokesman emerged to become an instant pop culture phenomenon—SPUDS MACKENZIE, "The Original Party Animal." SPUDS debuted in BUD LIGHT beer commercials that aired during SUPER BOWL XXI in 1987, and he quickly became the face of the brand. SPUDS was an English bull terrier who was a super cool, fun-loving, adventurous, beer-drinking partying dude! What he didn't have in good looks, he made up for with his quirkiness, charisma, swagger, and macho-man personality. Winning "best commercials of SUPER BOWL XXI", SPUDS was THE topic of conversation the next day.

He was an instant celebrity, and he turned the advertising and licensing worlds upside down! He was in high demand, and everyone wanted more of him. He did interviews with famous people like Dick Clark; had his own hotel room when he traveled; was always accompanied by three gorgeous ladies called the "Spudettes"; enjoyed riding in limousines, and wore a sharp black and white tuxedo during personal appearances. His *one job* was to increase BUD LIGHT sales and market share which he did as sales rose 20% during his reign. No one expected him to become a licensing star!!

When SPUDS-mania exploded, I was working in the Anheuser-Busch licensing department, and we were introduced to SPUDS along with all of America. What happened next was even more surprising! Monday morning, January 26, 1987 (the day after SUPER BOWL XXI), our phones rang off the wall. One of the first calls was from Macy's. While having a retailer support a licensed property is usually a licensor's dream, we were shocked. They announced Macy's would be launching the first SPUDS MACKENZIE Boutique at the Herald Square store in New York City the first week of April—only 10 weeks away! Purchase orders in hand for SPUDS MACKENZIE licensed merchandise, they also expected SPUDS to make a personal appearance! How was this going to happen when we had no warning, no licensing strategy, no style guide, and no retail licensed products? With the help of a very willing brand manager and eager licensees, we managed to outfit the store with limited inventory and great signage.

On April 7, 1987, the first SPUDS MACKENZIE Boutique opened at Macy's, and a huge crowd gathered to meet this surfboarding, skateboarding, rockstar of a dog. He arrived by limo (of course) with the 3 SPUDETTES and paparazzi everywhere! SPUDS was wearing shorts, a BUD LIGHT t-shirt and sunglasses—so cool! The store manager insisted on a picture with SPUDS for his office wall of other celebrity photos. SPUDS and his entourage then went to a special room (let's say it was his dressing room), where he changed into his tuxedo. With the SPUDETTES flanking him on each side, he walked into the "shop" and settled atop a tall director's chair with his name printed on the back. While people were lined up around the block to get a glimpse and maybe a picture with SPUDS, the excited store manager announced this was the biggest turnout for any celebrity appearance at Macy's ever!

Sadly, all good things must come to an end and SPUDS' time in the licensing and advertising limelight was short-lived. Like any truly, big star, controversy erupted. His personal life was put under the microscope, his gender questioned, his pedigree challenged (was he a dreaded Pit Bull?); and there were rumors that he died in a plane crash, in a limo accident or a hot tub incident. And, not everyone was a fan!! One year after SPUDS debuted, Senator Strom Thurmond stood before the Senate and accused Anheuser-Busch of using the SPUDS mascot ads and licensed products to sell alcohol to underage drinkers. Mothers Against Drunk Driving and other similar organizations supported the Senator's accusations and demanded action. This was not something the beer giant wanted to hear or to have to defend.

As SPUDS mania gripped the country, thousands of counterfeit products bearing his likeness including toys, baby clothes, and small size t-shirts showed up everywhere. The counterfeiters argued that SPUDS was just a cute, white dog; that no one owned this dog, and it was ok to print any size t-shirt with a cute, white dog and call him SPUDS MACKENZIE. Anheuser-Busch did not agree!! The company protects and defends its brands as well as prohibits any use of their brands for promotional purposes on children's products. While all the counterfeit items were illegal and had to be dealt with, the children's items added fuel to the firestorm brewing around accusations that SPUDS was promoting alcohol to children. The counterfeiters tried to disguise their products by including the BUD LIGHT logo and products, the SPUDS' signature and pawprint, and trademark and copyright notices, all of which were required on official licensed products. I was chosen as the A-B SPUDS MACKENZIE licensing representative to assist law enforcement officials in identifying and seizing counterfeit products. At one flea market alone, we seized over 10,000 counterfeit t-shirts!

Anheuser-Busch took strong legal actions to discontinue and remove these illegal products from the market and launched a responsible drinking ad campaign that moved away from the goofy, fun-loving antics of SPUDS. In 1989, claiming the character's image had begun to overshadow the brand, SPUDS was removed from the commercials, and his unforgettable licensing program ended as well.

We know licensing celebrities can be risky, and it is a shame the program ended so quickly. It was fun while it lasted, but it was the right decision even though SPUDS had no control over what was happening. The good news is SPUDS MACKENZIE will forever be "The Original Party Animal" and will remain one of the most unforgettable, beloved, coolest licensed brand mascots of all time! Cheers!

Arlene Scanlan on Rodney Dangerfield

Here is one that got away … and thank goodness for that! In 1989, as a licensing agent working at United Media, I was contacted by a talent agent who asked if I would be interested in meeting with Rodney Dangerfield. He had developed a children's animated feature called *Rover Dangerfield* and was looking for an agent to help develop both the film rights and the licensing rights. In the old days, things like that still happened. I agreed to meet with Rodney, and we confirmed a day and time, and I was given his home address to meet with him.

I brought along a gal that worked for me at the time as moral support. Rodney lived on the Upper East Side in a very tall building overlooking the East River. As soon as we arrived at the building, the doorman knew who we were and told us to go right up to Rodney's apartment.

We walked down a very long, carpeted hall and rang his doorbell. Rodney answered wearing a grey velour leisure-type suit. His red hair standing straight up, his bulging red eyes, and his big belly all were trademarks of the Rodney that we had seen on TV. We walked in and he offered us bottled water, a novel thing in those days so we said sure. He asked us to sit and wait in the living room which we did, and he proceeded to walk out of the room saying he would be back shortly.

10 minutes later he emerged but to our mutual shock and surprise, he was naked. Not a pretty sight but one burned into my brain to this day. We both stared and waited to see what he might say or do. He proceeded to sit down across the living room from us just a few feet away from where we could view his embarrassing package. To this day, I cannot say why we said nothing or what we were thinking but just like the emperor's new clothes, neither of us said a word about his being unclothed. We listened to him talk about his movie concept and listened to a couple of songs from the very cute movie, but I am not sure I could judge anything while I was sitting and looking at a naked Rodney Dangerfield.

My associate and I avoided eye contact with one another knowing if we did make eye contact, it was all over and would end in hysterical laughter. Suddenly we looked at each other and boom, we burst out laughing uncontrollably. Rodney seemed shocked. "What's so funny", he said. Trying to catch my breath, I finally said, "Bottled Water!" He seemed satisfied with that response and we held it together and regained our composure.

We stayed and talked for another half hour, unbelievably and then we said our goodbyes and left. We again broke into a huge laughing fit in the hallway, but once we caught our breath, we got in cabs and went our separate ways.

We did not rep Rover Dangerfield or Rodney and I view this as just one of those properties that did not make it to the roster!

Brian Hakan on Licensing with Kenny Rogers

I got to know Kenny Rogers quite well and had the pleasure to spend a lot of time with him when he was my client. We put three licensing deals together: a Kenny Rogers' THE GAMBLER slot machine; worldwide deals with IGT; and two book deals with Addax Publishing.

The Kenny Rogers I knew was a very genuine, nice man who treated those around him with respect and didn't take himself that seriously. I saw him make decisions from a third-party point of view. I recall a meeting with Kenny and his business partner, Jim Mazza, in their Dreamcatcher Studios Nashville offices, when I heard Kenny say in response to the suggestion that he promote his new "The

Greatest" book on an upcoming appearance on The Tonight Show, that "No, Kenny Rogers would never do that!"

The Greatest Song

I also recall the time after Kenny had just recorded his new song "The Greatest" about a little boy, a baseball, a bat, and a positive attitude written by Don Schlitz especially for Kenny. Don Schlitz also wrote, "The Gambler" which became a  hit for Kenny many years before, which also spawned into several HBO feature films as well. I suggested to my friends who ran The Super Show (which was the largest Trade Show in America at that time, comprised of 10+ Sports-Related Trade Shows, all housed together in the Georgia World Congress Center and The Georgia Dome at the same time each February in Atlanta) that Kenny perform this song at their annual sporting goods industry breakfast which was held in a convention center ballroom and attended by sporting goods executives, retailers, and their staff/guests. The stage was set up in a talk show-style set with the highly regarded sportswriter/sportscaster Dick Schaap as host. His guests were college and NBA basketball legend Bill Russell, as well as Kenny Rogers. When it was Kenny's turn, he pulled out his acoustic guitar and performed "The Greatest", about the young boy, his bat and a positive attitude as the outcome. In the end, the crowd roared its approval at its dramatic and positive conclusion.

Afterward, The Super Show management, with security, gave Kenny and his wife, Wanda and me a tour of the top sporting goods exhibits once the Super Show opened. We were able to meet the executives of the likes of ADIDAS, NIKE, RAWLINGS, WILSON, SPALDING, PUMA, and others. They each gave Kenny and Wanda comp stuff, as you can imagine, running shoes from one, tennis shoes from another, golf clubs, tennis rackets, warm-ups, and other clothing. We also had a serious conversation with the folks at RAWLINGS, who after witnessing Kenny's performance of "The Greatest" and its baseball-themed message earlier that morning and the audience's passionate response, suggested that they partner together to give away $150K of their sporting goods free to the BOYS AND GIRLS CLUBS across America.

So, Tim Richards, promotions guy for RAWLINGS, designed a program for Kenny to do a live, in-studio interview followed by a performance of "The Greatest" baseball song on the air with an announcement of their $10K gift of sporting goods to each local charity in 15 markets. Then Kenny would also perform it live at the local MLB ballpark after The National Anthem before the game started. Several of these 15 events were timed to occur on Opening Day in front of a full stadium. As you can imagine, Kenny and RAWLINGS built a lot of goodwill as well as sales of music and sporting goods as a result. We also developed a line of KENNY ROGERS'

THE GREATEST merchandise products consisting of an autographed baseball, cap, jersey, and bat all decorated with this new THE GREATEST/RAWLINGS logo.

The Gambler Slot Machine

Joe Kaminkow and Nancy King, executives at International Game Technology (IGT) met with Jim Mazza and me for dinner at the Las Vegas Hilton steakhouse before a Kenny Rogers performance at their main showroom. After our dinner, we met to discuss IGT's dominant position in the global slot machine industry as well as Kenny's global audience appeal and attended Kenny's sold-out performance, with the IGT folks appropriately seated front row center at the stage. Nancy and Joe along with the packed house experienced firsthand Kenny's professional yet very personal and passionate performance and the rousing response he received from his audience. We all were invited backstage to visit with Kenny in his dressing room, where we discussed his show, his audience, and our slot machine deal. Again, Kenny didn't take himself seriously and played the role of the engaging superstar entertainer who came across genuinely and friendly in his inimitable, natural and quite endearing way again from his egoless third-party point of view. He took an active role in discussing and closing our deal which went on to enjoy international sales for its 10+ year run.

The Toy Shoppe

Kelly Junkermann, who co-wrote and directed "The Toy Shoppe" with Kenny, and wrote the music and performed the lead role of Hang Longley during this perennial highly-acclaimed and well-loved family favorite Christmas show, helped pull together another magical evening with Kenny Rogers. We put the book deal together, including the original songs written and performed by Kenny on a CD that was included in a sleeve attached to the inside back book cover. That way, the reader could listen to Kenny perform these songs, which were integral to the moving story about Christmas Miracles, as they read along to follow the story.

We invited Don Hall, Chairman of Hallmark Cards, and his wife, Adele, who is a huge Kenny Rogers fan, to attend the Kansas City performance of "The Toy Shoppe". Hallmark was considering sponsoring a television broadcast of "The Toy Shoppe". Kenny's annual Christmas tour started with a performance of "The Toy Shoppe story" complete with its Hero and Bruno plush dog character sand disabled toy role model, who both come to life, where Kenny played the role of Hank Longley and sang the songs with the ensemble, of course with the requisite happy ending including the Christmas Miracle. Then, after an intermission where Kenny changed into his Kenny Rogers superstar entertainer attire, he mesmerized his audience with one after another of his myriad of hits to satisfy the appetite of his adoring audience. Before the show, the Halls and my Dad, Mel, and his wife, Ro as well as our son, Daniel were treated to a very warm and enjoyable photo op backstage with Kenny, who always seemed to enjoy it as much as his fans.

In 1999, I was invited to join Kenny and his management team to attend the inaugural introduction of the new designation of the Diamond Album sales level at NYC's Roseland Ballroom of Kenny Rogers' Greatest Hits, which was one of only a few albums that had sold more than 10 million albums at that time.

In 2000, at Arrowhead Stadium, to celebrate KC150, Kansas City's Sesquicentennial Event, Kenny headlined with Walter Cronkite, a KC area native as the MC. Little Richard and others were there as well. Again, Kenny was so generous with his time, showing little Daniel around his limo before his performance as well as meeting and posing backstage for photos with friends, clients and VIPs alike, always so respectful of other's time and generally always appearing gracious and genuine in his interaction with others.

RIP, Kenny, you'll live on forever in your stories through your songs. You've shown an amazing knack for selecting songs that allow you to tell your stories in your most genuine, personal, and respectful way to your audience. I consider myself blessed to have had the privilege to know you personally and professionally as we were able to work together to make a difference in others' lives, and our own, and to have had the real pleasure to share some time together. Thank you, sweet music man, for decorating our lives with yours.

Jay Foreman on Dealing with Hollywood Stars

Jay Foreman, currently president of Basic Fun and a veteran of the toy industry at companies including Play Along, Galoob, Hasbro and the Bridge, recounts his experiences with the following celebrities:

- BRITNEY SPEARS: I used 50% of the startup capital we had raised to put up a $1.5m advance for rights to a 16-year-old emerging pop star! 1999. We ended up doing huge business, but it was a big risk on an unknown teenager! Play Along might never have gotten off the ground if she bombed out or got caught smoking a joint!
- SPICE GIRLS: I Flew to London to meet with Simon Fueller, manager of the Spice Girls who later created American Idol. He left us waiting outside the gate of his country estate for 30 minutes in the hot sun for a meeting. Then

he made us sit out on a blanket on the lawn for a garden meeting while, in between, he left for 40 minutes to go inside to get acupuncture on his back! Total rock-and-roll meeting. Fortunately, we got the deal and the next day met and worked with all the girls.

- CABBAGE PATCH Kids: We re-launched the property in 2004 at the Mall of America with Xavier Roberts and our host and MC, Paula Abdul. The first stage was a morning press conference followed by an afternoon meet and greet. Paula had taken a red eye from LA and was still hungover from the sleeping pills that she took on the plane. She literally couldn't function for the press conference. We had to postpone it and let her sleep in the limo in the garage. When she woke up and snapped out of it in the afternoon for the event and meet and greet, she was fabulous, but it was touch and go all the way.

Celebrity Shorts

Dealing with celebrities in the context of licensing can be challenging, primarily because it is a world that they are not necessarily accustomed to working in. Some of the stories can be uplifting and encouraging, while others can be downright head shaking, for example:

A famous Hollywood actress approved her image for use on a movie poster and tie-in book associated with her next blockbuster film, but then changed her mind because she decided she looked "fat" in the photo. This resulted in the destruction of 50,000 paperbacks. Now, this A-lister probably weighed 100 pounds soaking wet, and most women would cut off an arm to look like her. But never underestimate an actress who thinks she looks fat and a movie studio who wants to keep her happy.

****

Another favorite story also involved a famous Hollywood personality who became involved in litigation. The other side had requested that the celebrity's deposition be taken by video. The request was opposed by the celebrity's counsel because of the possibility that the video could be pirated, uploaded, and go viral. The judge in the case understood the possible ramifications and ordered that the deposition be taken in the courthouse with a retired judge present to supervise the proceedings and deal with any objections, etc. that might arise.

As luck would have it, the celebrity decided to go out and party the night before the deposition and, as a result, appeared late for the deposition and somewhat under the weather. It started with the celebrity kissing the judge on his lips, prompting him to say, "That is the first time in my career that a witness has ever kissed me!" The room burst out laughing.

After numerous stops and starts, the celebrity asked for a recess to compose herself, after apparently drinking Red Bull most of the day with no food and throwing up in the bathroom. That brought the proceeding to a swift conclusion.

The retired judge turned to the celebrity's counsel and said, "We would have finished this deposition and gone home hours ago if your client wasn't such a dingbat."

****

Then there was the story of another Hollywood actress who was approached about representing a jewelry manufacturer in exchange for a mid-seven-figure endorsement fee. One of the conditions of the request was that she would be required to wear the manufacturer's jewelry on the red carpet to help promote it. In the negotiations, she balked, saying, "what happens if I don't like the jewelry? Can I design my own?" This came from a young actress whose knowledge of jewelry design was about as much as her knowledge of rocket science.

Dell Furano on how Marvel "Kiss Comic" Used Real Blood in Ink

Dell Furano of Epic Rights is one of the legends of the licensing industry, particularly concerning the representation of music groups. He is a member of LIMA's Licensing Hall of Fame. He relates the following story involving KISS.

In 1977 Marvel Comics published Super Special KISS full-color comic book presenting the band as superheroes. In order to commemorate the launch of the comic book, it was decided that the ink to be used to print the first issue would contain blood from each KISS band member.

In order to achieve this result, blood from each band member was drawn by a registered nurse, witnessed by a notary public, and poured into the vats of red ink used for printing the comic at Marvel's Borden Ink plant in Depew, New York.

Commenting on the process, Gene Simmons said, "As the Kiss comic book project moved along, someone came up with the idea of putting real blood in the ink. It wasn't me. We got into a DC3, one of those big prop planes, and flew up to Buffalo to Marvel's printing plant, where they pour the ink and make comic books. A notary public actually witnessed the blood being drawn."

Below is the letter from the notary. It reads, "This is to certify that KISS members, Gene Simmons, Ace Frehley, Paul Stanley, and Peter Criss, have each donated blood which is being collectively mixed with the red ink to be used for the first issue of the Marvel/KISS comic. The blood was extracted on February 21st, 1977 at Nassau Coliseum and has been under guarded refrigeration until this day when it was delivered to the Borden Ink plant in Depew, New York."

This is to certify that KISS members, Gene
Simmons, Ace Frehley, Paul Stanley and Peter
Criss, have each donated blood which is being
collectively mixed with the red ink to be
used for the first issue of the Marvel/KISS
Comics. The blood was extracted on February
21st, 1977 at Nassau Coliseum and has been
under guarded refrigeration until this day
when it was delivered in an armored truck
to the Borden Ink plant in Depew, New York.

AUCOIN

Before me this 26th day of May, 1977, came
Gene Simmons, Ace Frehley, Paul Stanley and
Peter Criss, being known to me and known as
the persons who signed the foregoing instrument
and did so declare.

State of _New York_

County of _Suffolk_

Notary Public

Not the first time KISS has done something out of the ordinary regarding marketing. They also made limited edition KISS caskets and "Dimebag" Darrell was buried in one.

XII. Licensing Strands

by Robert Strand

A Sign That It's Over

As an eager young assistant buyer at FAO Schwarz who had just learned how to do key item forecasting – in the early 1990s when you used an excel spreadsheet, hand wrote purchase orders and snail-mailed them (we eventually justified investing in a fax machine)– I was given the task of re-ordering the exclusive Nicole Miller for FAO print; this meant determining out of a minimum number of yards of fabric how many silk bomber jackets, sarong skirts, cummerbund & bow tie kits, etc. you were going to order.

I remember it was quite an investment, and shortly before the order was to arrive, I noticed something and went to my boss, Connie Van Epps, and said, "I think the Nicole Miller thing might be over." "Why?" she asked, to which I replied, "Well, I saw our silk bomber on a homeless person this morning."

****

NBA Finals v. LIMA Awards Ceremony

In 2003, the San Antonio Spurs and the New Jersey Nets were in the Finals, and I was Senior Director of all Fan Licensed Products, which meant that I had 108 licensees who did up to 60% of their annual volume in the window during the NBA Playoffs and Finals.

In a weekly Global Merchandising Group staff meeting, our leader Sal LaRocca stated, "For those of you who have lobbied LIMA to acknowledge sports licensing in the licensing community, congratulations. I just got off the phone with Charles Riotto over at LIMA, and he HIGHLY suggested that someone – one of you – be at the LIMA awards ceremony next week "just in case."

Hands were not flying up around the room, but I saw an opportunity and said I would do it. The opportunity was going to be having a little fun at the expense of Ross Auerbach at The Northwest Company ... and I could not wait.

Ross had been asking me for an exclusive license for almost a year which was something I couldn't grant. At the NBA, exclusive licensing partnerships were reserved for those that committed to marketing partnerships and a licensing partnership – and things that were game-related. What he did not know was that there were other things I was willing to negotiate, but that is not the point of this story.

I go to the 2003 Gala, which was the first LIMA (now Licensing International) event that I attended. I sit with Ross Auerbach and the Northwest team knowing he would bring up the topic of our contract renewal, which he did like clockwork. So, I started to counter with, "You know Ross, I don't know that you believe in the power of the NBA, in what it stands for and what it can mean to your company. He visibly started to get defensive and upset, almost taking it personally, trying again to sell me on the importance of exclusivity, that he is a believer!"

Meanwhile, I've just been biding my time, waiting for the moment, and this time I have my timing perfect. I look at Ross, gently touch him on the shoulder, look him square in the eye, and say, "Ross, hold that thought." And from the stage the announcer says:

"And the award for best sports brand goes to the NBA!" I look at Ross and say, "I'll be right back".

When I got back to my seat the look on Ross's face was worth missing that Spurs-Nets Finals game for, and we ended up negotiating a fair deal.

****

Micromanagement is Underrated

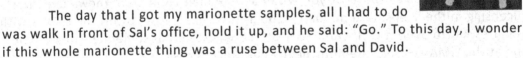

In 2002, David Stern and his wife Diane returned from a trip to Portugal *convinced* that NBA Player Marionette puppets would sell like *"hotcakes."* In charge of "fan licensed products," I was put in charge of sourcing. My boss, Sal LaRocca, looked at me and said, "I know … just … do it." Periodically, if Sal or I bumped into David in the elevator or at the NBA Café, he would ask about his puppets. Mind you, David had this encyclopedic memory that, without missing a beat, could go from the ridiculous to the most complex of topics in a nanosecond with incredible fluidity.

The day that I got my marionette samples, all I had to do was walk in front of Sal's office, hold it up, and he said: "Go." To this day, I wonder if this whole marionette thing was a ruse between Sal and David.

The day I got my samples happened to be the day before the annual, end-of-season picnic for the 2001/02 season. It was *also* a day when David's office was very "enthusiastic" about TV broadcast rights discussions. Negotiation strategies were happening — with a variety of colorful superlatives being shouted – I mean discussed (this was when the league went with ESPN/ABC valued at $2.4B over NBC's $1.3B).

So, as I walked into David's office as these discussions were unfolding, the superlatives started to fly, and I'm holding this stupid puppet. Discretion being the better part of valor, I decided that I should come back later, so I got up to leave. Suddenly David shouts, "Wait a minute. wait a minute!" Now I'm freaking out thinking he's seen me trying to escape, but David continues, "It's HOT! What are those water mist things that people walk under to stay cool? Get Events on the phone! I want those water mist things at my picnic tomorrow. None of my people are going to die of heatstroke! Not on my watch!"

We called the Events staff, and I confirmed that the water mist things would be in place the next day. Without missing a beat, David went straight back into negotiations. Loud negotiations.

I left the puppet with David's assistant, Linda Toss, and whispered, "I'll come back another time." She replied, "If you value your life."

****

Challenges to Licensing Interns

Every summer at the NBA when I was Sr. Director of Non-Apparel Licensing, I would get an intern and would challenge that intern to find a PR value deal to learn the licensing process. They had to not only find it but bind the deal before their internship was up. Two of my favorites include a "Personality" and a "Celebrity."

Tip: Meet your "Personality" Licensee *Before* the Day You Appear Together Live on ESPN

In 2004, my intern, Ciji-Danielle Robinson, insisted that we license Jacob the Jeweler to do a diamond-encrusted NBA five-time zone watch. I am not a complete nerd, but I admit I am not well versed in hip-hop slang, I had no idea what dressing dip-down, fly even means, and I will never be able to pull off the bling.

Ciji got the license done and the deal became newsworthy as was the goal. It's worth noting that I had only met Jacob the Jeweler's (real name Jacob Arabo) business manager at this point. ESPN2's *Cold Pizza* wanted to interview Jacob and me, so the date was set and the first time that I met Jacob was on the *Cold Pizza* set.

Jacob is an Uzbek-born American widely known as "Jacob the Jeweler" or "King of Bling", but English is not his first language and his personality belies the sparkle of his title. We sat down on set, and this very bubbly and articulate woman interviewing us lists all these facts about his company which sets Jacob up to tell his story. She looks at him and says, "So a lot of NBA players wear your watches?!"

After a momentary pause, on live television, in his thick Uzbek accent, he says, "Yes." That was it. That was all he said.

****

Remember Michigan J. Frog?

Do you Remember Michigan J. Frog, the singing frog from LOONEY TUNES where the light goes on and he lets out one ribbit? That is what Jacob sounded like. I think I chimed in with something like, "At the NBA we want our fans to connect with the game through unique and relevant products. Jacob is being modest; players proudly wear his watches which is why we've licensed them…"

P.S. Two years later, he went to prison for lying to federal investigators about a multimillion-dollar drug ring.

****

I Should Have Trademarked That

One summer my intern, Tara Schwartz, noticed female African-American celebrities being photographed at Laker games wearing "China Moon Rags." They were Swarovski crystal bejeweled bandana headbands by comedic actress Tichina Arnold. So, we called her into the NYC league office to talk to her about an NBA license so that she could make a legit Lakers do-rag for Shaq's mom.

I could tell she was nervous, and meanwhile, I was like, "I have 'Pam from *Martin*' in my office." I asked her if she knew much about basketball and she sheepishly said, "No." I replied, "Good. I was recruited after JORDAN retired because I did not come from sports. Despite being tall, I know nothing about basketball – that's what my interns are for." She fell off her chair laughing and said she would sign anything I wanted her to sign.

The next year, the NBA launched the sub-brand NBA4Her and there was a launch event. GIII was the apparel licensee and a few models were going to wear Tichina's bejeweled do-rags. So she and I drove over to the event in her car in Manhattan. That is when it got fun.

Tichina was wearing this leather top, that she had never tried on before. It only buttoned on the top of the left shoulder, so as we are driving across midtown Manhattan, her right breast kept popping out of her shirt. Tichina was playing a new Missy Elliot CD and the song as her right breast was dancing all over the place was, and I apologize if this offends anyone, "Pu$$y Don't Fail Me Now".

I looked at Tichina and said, "You do realize that every straight man and lesbian on the planet hates me right now, right?" I don't know how she drove because we were laughing so hard. Just then, this sassy, fabulous NBA colleague, Joannitte Rodriguez Questell (Isn't that a great name), "ROBERRRRT! Where you two at?! You're missing all the titty action with this fashion show. Come on!" To which I replied, "Joannitte, I've had my very own celebrititty action allll night. Meet me with some double stick tape at the front door."

Celebrititty. I should have trademarked that.

****

He's Trying to Waist Our Time

The Vice President of Licensing at K2 Inc (the holding company with 29 sporting goods and technical apparel brands) was not, I remember, excited about having a "corporate resource" to help evaluate licensing for the NBA4Her brand.

After a few conversations with K2 Sports (who deeply resented the parent company using "their" name), I realized that they were one division that really did not want help. When my boss asked me why I felt that way, I said that the K2 Sports president wants me to prioritize an apparel licensing strategy for their snowshoe brand, Tubbs. The boss didn't seem to understand, to which I asked him to find me one woman who wants to wear Tubbs branded apparel.

****

Ain't Too Proud to Beg

One person's trash is another's treasure. In December 1996, I joined Motown Café, a licensee of Motown, as Director of Merchandise. After my orientation, I was told that the environment was in fact a hostile work environment; if you were a little person, tall, straight, gay, Catholic, Jewish "we rip on everyone."

There was true love and support in the fun that was made, and despite the odds, we were profitable. "Bring it," was my delighted response.

After that orientation, I was told that I inherited a nine-year supply of these grey microphone banks that normally would hold a t-shirt rolled up inside. Six-Flags Theme Parks was a sister company and had helped with the merchandising before I was hired, and this concept worked well, for them.

As a true merchant, I experimented with different ways to move the banks and committed to my boss that I would find a way to sell them while maintaining my 29% cost margin. I found a company to make me gummy microphones, put 12-ounce bags of the gummy mic's in them, and sold that entire inventory in eighteen months.

One afternoon I went into my boss's office wanting to re-order the banks. Items I dodged fleeing from his office included a pen, a staple gun, a padfolio, and a paperweight.

XIII. How I Got Started in Licensing

Basic Fun's First License—SUPER SOAKER

Alan Dorfman recalls that the first license that he ever pursued was for a SUPER SOAKER keychain. Alan had worked for Larami, a Philadelphia based toy company, when the product that became SUPER SOAKER, was under development. He would then leave Larami to start his own toy company called Impulse Toys at the time when the SUPER SOAKER water blasters were the hottest, best-selling water toys in the world. He had maintained good ties with the people at Larami, including Al Davis, one of the owners, and a mentor to him. After several months of pestering Al with his idea, Davis called him one day and told him that they had hired a licensing agency to represent the SUPER SOAKER brand and that he should pitch his concept to them. The agency was then called LCI but would later change its name to 4 Kids which became the licensing agency of POKÉMON, YU GI OH, CABBAGE PATCH KIDS, and many other very successful brands.

Alan contacted them and was told to submit a proposal, which he did. A meeting was set up for them to see what other products Alan's new company, Basic Fun, was doing.

So, at a little, rented corner of a showroom in the Toy Building at 200 Fifth Avenue, Alan had a meeting with Cynthia from LCI. It lasted less than a minute. Cynthia rushed in, looked at his skirted folding table of assorted open market tchotchkes, looked at him, and said, "ee cc hh". Without another word, she turned and left. End of the meeting.

Later, Alan would call Al Davis to thank him for the opportunity and tell him that he didn't think they would be giving him a license. He told Al about the "meeting" and was told not to worry about it. A few weeks later, Alan received a contract from LCI for SUPER SOAKER keychains.

Despite having little experience, Alan was able to work with contacts in Hong Kong and have a great product built. He had two models of SUPER SOAKER keychains manufactured, based on the first two models of SUPER SOAKER — the SUPER SOAKER 50 and SUPER SOAKER 100. And the best part was that they worked. When you  pulled back on the barrel, they squirted a stream of water surprisingly far for their small size and more shots than you would expect.

SUPER SOAKER was now well established as the must-have water blaster, and SUPER SOAKER keychains were an instant hit. Basic Fun sold over 5,000,000 units in the first year. At one point, they were the #3 top-selling toy in the country.

Basic Fun was a 3-person company and had a *bona fide* home run of a product on the market. Every morning, Alan would open the office and the fax machine would be out of paper from all the orders the had come in overnight (pre-email)!

By the next Spring, Cynthia and LCI had nominated SUPER SOAKER keychains for the LIMA's Licensed Hardgoods product of the year. Cynthia escorted Alan into the awards ceremony, her arm wrapped around his, and escorted him to his "reserved for nominee seat" in the front. Alan said that he felt like he was at the Academy Awards. SUPER SOAKER did not win that year, it lost to what was the #1 toy line of the year, POWER RANGERS by Bandai.

Basic Fun went on to run with the concept of miniaturizing toys onto keychains. Keychains went from a throwaway category, without a real home at retail, to a destination category of toy departments all over. It started churning them out, first toys, then entertainment properties, and other well-known products. Kids could not get enough of them, and to show off their collections, they began displaying them by hanging them on their backpacks. To this day, when you see a keychain adorning a backpack, the roots of that are in that first Basic Fun SUPER SOAKER keychain.

Licensing at a Toy Company is Like Nowhere Else

John McCann, a former Hasbro counsel, reflects on his introduction into licensing at Hasbro with the following story: I had recently been hired as an in-house licensing attorney at Hasbro when the head of the department decided that, henceforth, new license requests that came in would be assigned to the next lawyer on a list. As a result, I had been assigned a contract for an item named "Bada Bing Bada Boom" (this item predated "The Sopranos"). The licensor of the item was a long-time, experienced toy inventor who had previously placed numerous items with the company. After my initial contact with the inventor, he had contacted his attorney with whom he had done his previous agreement and asked if he could just use that form for the new item. The other attorney had said that would be fine.

When I heard this from the inventor, I asked my department head if this would be okay. He immediately confronted the other attorney and said: "This is John's file. You had no right to tell the inventor he could use "Giggle Wiggle" for "Bada Bing Bada Boom." At that moment I knew that working at a toy company wasn't like in-house work elsewhere.

Licensing Sure Beats Patent Prosecution

Greg Battersby recounted his early days in licensing in the legal department at Gulf + Western Industries which, at the time, owned Paramount Pictures, Madison Square Garden, Kayser Roth Hosiery, and a hundred other companies. He had joined G+W as Associate Patent Counsel, coming from two major IP firms in New York. He had been originally recruited to perform a range of patent activities for various subsidiaries as well as several government contracts issues.

As luck would have it, the attorney on his left was Bruce Hosmer, who did much of the Paramount licensing work. While Greg was toiling away on mundane patent "stuff," Bruce was doing "fun stuff" like attending STAR TREK conventions and overseeing much of the licensing activities. Ten years later, Bruce would become LIMA's first general counsel only to be replaced by Greg after his untimely demise.

On the other side of Greg was G+W's trademark counsel, initially Chuck Grimes and later, Howard Barnaby. Their role, among others, was to file trademark applications for Paramount's various merchandising marks. In furtherance of his activities, they would regularly receive cases of samples of licensed merchandise,

e.g., MORK & MINDY T-shirts, STAR TREK action figures, GREASE sweatshirts, etc. to support the trademark applications. They were receiving so many samples of merchandise that it seems as if they were running a sample shop out of their office, supplying Greg and other G+W lawyers and their families with cutting edge samples for themselves and their kids. Greg's young children were regularly attired in MORK & MINDY t-shirts and STAR TREK jackets.

It didn't take very long for Greg to decide that merchandising and licensing were much more fun than writing patent applications for such exciting things as cotton crotch pantyhose, locking bolts for caskets, or slot cars for Sega.

That led to Greg taking on more of the merchandising responsibilities and ultimately co-authoring an article with Chuck Grimes on the "Protection of Merchandising Properties" which was published by the *Trademark Reporter* by the U.S. Trademark Association (now International Trademark Association) in 1979. The pair would eventually leave G+W in the early 1980s and form a new law firm ultimately called Grimes & Battersby, which developed a specialty in licensing.

Kalle Torma Breaking in with Angry Birds

The Nordics are well known for a lot of things: stunning natural landscapes, the northern lights, and creating Santa Claus, among others. One thing the region is not known for, however, is licensing. In 2018, I was determined to change that.

Let me give you a bit of backstory: I started my company, Flowhaven, in 2016, as a young, hungry entrepreneur interested in building a state-of-the-art licensing relationship management (LRM) platform that would help brand licensing professionals grow and scale. By 2018, I had numerous stamps in my passport, secured by traveling the world over to learn everything I could about the business and ensuring that the product I was building served every need. My trip to North America was especially illuminating, where I attended the Licensing Expo and met the deal makers and creators who were responsible for turning the properties that inspired me to enter the business into global sensations.

That is when the lightbulb went off! I needed a way to bring American expertise to the Nordics, where audiences were growing increasingly hungry for licensed merchandise based on mobile games, anime, and blockbuster films. At that point, Nordic licensing was in its infancy and largely applied to our local fashion and tech communities. Within weeks, my co-founder and I organized "Insights to North American Brand Licensing and Merchandising" a one-day event that we hoped would include Anita  Castellar, CEO Fangirl Licensing; Andrew Lawrence, former licensing director, Pyramid America; author and thought leader Pete Canalichio; and Michael Melby, director, consumer products, Crunchyroll. They were all industry titans with a wealth of knowledge.

There were only two problems: How would we convince the speakers to travel 12,000+ miles for a one-day event? Some had never been to Finland, or even to Europe. How would we get our local audience fired up about the conference? My team had to learn in real-time. The qualities I saw as negatives, quickly became strengths. In addition to selling the opportunity to visit one of the most beautiful places on earth, I pointed out the opportunity to present a holistic, friendly approach to licensing to a group hungry for knowledge. Maura Regan, the president of Licensing International, even agreed to attend. For the potential attendees, we became a two-man marketing team, adapting American concepts for the local audience and empowering them to think beyond their borders.

On the day of the event, I held my breath as I watched the two worlds collide. My confidence was a bit shaken as our coffee failed to arrive on time, a bad sign in a country obsessed with coffee and precision. As the speeches got underway, I realized that there was nothing to fear. We helped the audience understand the power of Licensing International, underscored the importance of relationship building, and provided key insights that changed the way the region engages in licensing.

The audience and speakers connected right away with many making connections that stand today. Two years later, the Nordics have contributed more than $4.8 billion to the licensing community. I feel confident saying we played some small role in that. Today, the speakers still tell me attending the conference was one of the best trips that they have ever taken. Even if our coffee obsession and quirks about crossing the sidewalk still puzzle them.

Louise Q. Caron – Colgate-Palmolive's Loss Was LCA's Gain

Louise Q. Caron, LIMA's former Sr. Vice President/Member Relations, was their very first employee and spent 33 years with the Association.

Before joining LIMA on Opening Day in 1985, Louise spent three years at Licensing Corp. of America, a division of Warner Communications – now Time Warner, Inc.

She recounts how she "stumbled" into licensing. Louise had been on an interview at Colgate-Palmolive on Park Avenue in New York City. Afterward, she stopped by Warner Communications at 75 Rockefeller Plaza to drop off her resume – no appointment – just walked in! She was asked if she had time to meet with an HR rep. Before she knew it, she was taking a typing test then off to meet the team at LCA. Two hours later, Louise was walking out of 75 Rock as a new employee of Licensing Corp. of America! It was her very first professional job out of college. She was so excited that she ran all the way to Penn Station – she couldn't wait to board the train to the Jersey Shore and tell her family the fabulous news. Remember … there were no cell phones back then. When Louise walked into the house, her Mom had big news for her … Colgate-Palmolive had called – she got the job! Too late.

Louise recalls that LCA was a great start to her professional career. She learned a lot in her three years there and felt she was prepared to go anywhere she chose after her training with the company. Murray Altchuler – her boss at LCA, and LIMA's co-founder/first Executive Director – invited her to join him when LIMA opened for business in the summer of 1985. She loved working with Murray, although she didn't have a lot of confidence that LIMA would get off the ground. She gave it a go, however, but she thought that she would probably be heading back to the Warner Communications conglomerate in two years. Who knew – 33 years later, LIMA was going strong, and Louise was still there!

Through the years, Louise wore many hats for the Association and worked on many programs. (LIMA was a two-person office for the first 12 years.) She loved the licensing industry and considered herself very fortunate to be a part of it. As she looks back on LIMA and what it has become, she's very proud to say she was there on Day One and was an integral part of its' success. In conclusion, she said it was a pleasure to work with LIMA CEO's, Murray Altchuler and Charles Riotto, and LIMA's Counsel, Greg Battersby, who she has always admired.

XIV. Cool Trademarks & Patents

Trademark Filings/Registrations
Sports-Themed

19-0 for clothing et al. by Kraft Group filed before 2007 SUPER BOWL anticipating a Patriots win

18-1 for Clothing by New York Post after the Patriots lost the 2007 SUPER BOWL

Tom Terrific for t-shirts by TEB Capital Management (Tom Brady)

Tampa Brady for clothing by TEB Capital Management

TB 12 for clothing by TEB Capital Management

Gronk for baseball caps by GronkNation

Just a Kid from Akron for clothing by LBJ Enterprises (LeBron James)

Celebrities

Sarah Palin for websites and educational materials by Sarah Palin…. after her original application was rejected because she forgot to sign her name

You're Fired! The Donald for men's cologne by New Horizons

Meredith, Olivia & Benjamin Swift (the names of Taylor Swift's cats) for clothing, etc. by TAS Trademarks

That's Hot for multimedia services by Paris Hilton

I Die for clothing by Rachel Zoe, Inc.

Rise and Shine for clothing, etc. by Kylie Jenner

OKURRR for clothing by Washpoppin (Cardi B)

Let's Get Ready to Rumble for clothing, coffee cups, etc. by Ready to Rumble, Inc. (Michael Buffer). Rumor has it that Buffer received more than $400M in royalties.

Colleges

The for clothing by The Ohio State University

Blue Turf for Entertainment Services by Boise State University

Hook 'em Horn for shirts and tank tops by Univ. of Texas

Orange for clothing etc. by Syracuse University

These Are Trademarks???

Sound of Revving Engine for motorcycles by Harley Davidson

WHASSUP for clothing by Anheuser-Busch

Sound of Beer Can Opening for clothing by Anheuser-Busch

Devil Horn's hand gesture for entertainment services by Gene Simmons

Sound of Darth Vader's Breath for Halloween costumes by Lucasfilm

Dun Dun Sound for Law & Order for entertainment services by NBC

COVID Couch Potato for fitness program by K.O.L.A. Inc.

Cool Patents

Classic Toys

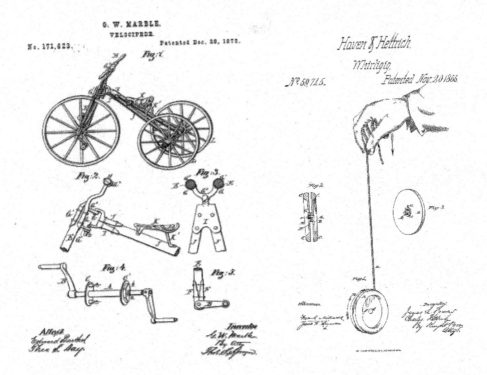

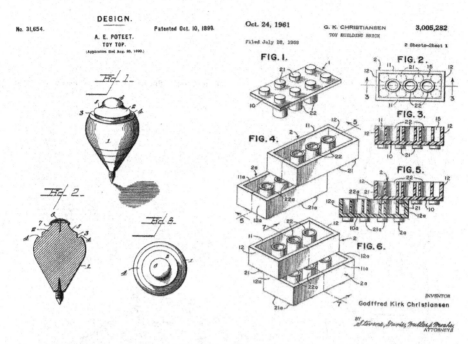

Iconic Products

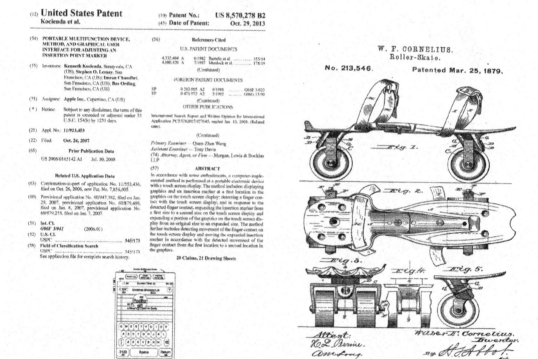

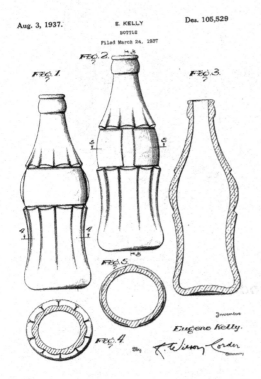

Aug. 3, 1937.　　　E. KELLY　　　Des. 105,529

BOTTLE

Filed March 24, 1937

FIG. 1.　　FIG. 2.　　FIG. 3.

FIG. 5.

FIG. 4.

Inventor

Eugene Kelly.

By R. Wilson Corder
(Attorney)

United States Patent [19]

Hatfield

[11]　Patent Number:　Des. 320,498

[45]　Date of Patent:　** Oct. 8, 1991

[54]　SHOE UPPER

[75]　Inventor:　Tinker L. Hatfield, Portland, Oreg.

[73]　Assignee:　Nike, Inc., Beaverton, Oreg.; Nike International Ltd., Bermuda

[**]　Term:　14 Years

[21]　Appl. No.: 558,415

[22]　Filed:　Jul. 27, 1990

[52]　U.S. Cl. D2/314; D2/312

[58]　Field of Search D2/264, 265, 268, 271,
D2/308–314; 36/45, 83, 84, 89, 102–106,
112–116, 132, 136

[56]　References Cited

U.S. PATENT DOCUMENTS

D. 261,751	1/1982	Anderie	D2/310
D. 272,964	3/1984	Feigelstock	D2/310
D. 283,461	4/1986	Channing	D2/310
D. 284,039	6/1986	Yoshitake	D2/310
D. 292,945	12/1987	Selbiger et al.	D2/314
D. 293,970	2/1988	Brown et al.	D2/314
D. 295,230	4/1988	Tong	D2/314
D. 295,458	6/1988	Selbiger	D2/314
D. 296,381	6/1988	Selbiger	D2/314
D. 297,181	8/1988	Selbiger et al.	D2/314
D. 297,587	9/1988	Selbiger et al.	D2/314
D. 297,882	10/1988	Tong et al.	D2/314
D. 299,081	12/1988	Greenberg	D2/314
D. 300,983	5/1989	Le	D2/314
D. 302,898	8/1989	Greenberg	D2/314
D. 308,577	1/1990	Felter et al.	D2/314

D. 307,663	5/1990	Boucher et al.	D2/314
4,577,419	3/1986	Channing	36/89
4,776,111	10/1988	Crowley	36/114

OTHER PUBLICATIONS

Nike Fall 1987 catalog–pp. 50, 52, 54.
Nike Fall 1988 catalog–pp. 60, 62, 64, 66.
Nike Spring 1989 catalog–pp. 62, 64, 66, 68.
Nike Fall 1989 catalog–pp. 54, 56, 58, 60.
Nike Spring 1990 catalog–pp. 56, 58, 60, 62, 64, 66.
Nike Fall 1990 catalog–pp. 56, 58, 60, 62, 64, 66.

Primary Examiner—Louis S. Zarfas
Attorney, Agent, or Firm—Banner, Birch, McKie & Beckett

[57]　CLAIM

The ornamental design for a shoe upper, as shown and described.

DESCRIPTION

FIG. 1 is a side elevational view of one side of a shoe upper showing my new design;
FIG. 2 is a side elevational view of the other side of the shoe upper shown in FIG. 1;
FIG. 3 is a front elevational view of the shoe upper shown in FIG. 1;
FIG. 4 is a rear elevational view of the shoe upper shown in FIG. 1; and
FIG. 5 is a top plan view of the shoe upper shown in FIG. 1.
The broken line showing of a shoe sole, including the warped vertical sides of the sole, is for illustrative purposes and forms no part of the claimed design.

Dolls & Figures

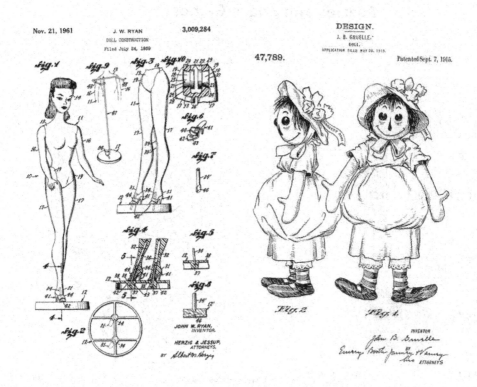

Nov. 21, 1961   J. W. RYAN   3,009,284
DOLL CONSTRUCTION
Filed July 24, 1959

JOHN W. RYAN,
INVENTOR.

HERZIG & JESSUP,
ATTORNEYS,
BY Albert M. Herzig

DESIGN.
J. B. GRUELLE.
DOLL.
APPLICATION FILED MAY 28, 1915.

47,789.   Patented Sept. 7, 1915.

INVENTOR
John B. Gruelle
Emery Booth Janney & Varney
his ATTORNEYS

Puzzles and Board Games

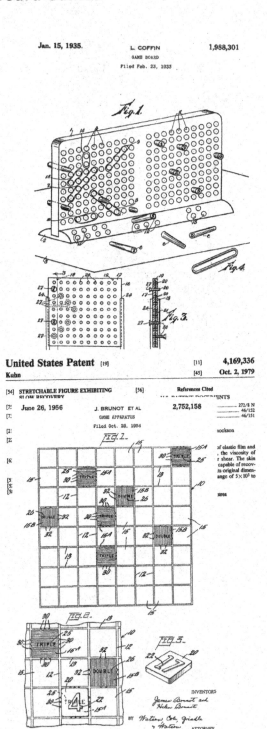

Dec. 31, 1935.   C. B. DARROW   2,026,082
BOARD GAME APPARATUS
Filed Aug. 31, 1935   7 Sheets-Sheet 1

Jan. 15, 1935.   L. COFFIN   1,988,301
GAME BOARD
Filed Feb. 23, 1933

United States Patent [19]
Rubik   [11] 4,378,116
                         [45] Mar. 29, 1983

[54] SPATIAL LOGICAL TOY

[75] Inventor: Ernö Rubik, Budapest, Hungary

[73] Assignee: Politoys Ipari Szövetkezet, Budapest, Hungary

[21] Appl. No.: 289,192

[22] Filed: Aug. 3, 1981

[30] Foreign Application Priority Data

Oct. 28, 1980 [HU] Hungary 2591/80

[51] Int. Cl. A63F 9/08
[52] U.S. Cl. .... 273/153 S
[58] Field of Search .... 273/153 S, 155

[56] References Cited
FOREIGN PATENT DOCUMENTS
170062 2/1978 Hungary .... 273/153 S

OTHER PUBLICATIONS
Scientific American, Mar. 1981, p. 39.

Primary Examiner—Anton O. Oechsle
Attorney, Agent, or Firm—Gabriel P. Katona

[57] ABSTRACT

A spatial logical toy is formed from a total of eighteen toy elements, out of which two sets of eight identical toy elements two connecting elements are provided. The elements of the two sets have cam members with hollows with spherical convex or concave surfaces in-between. The elements are connected by the aid of the cams and the two remaining centrally positioned substantially identical connecting elements each having a T-shape cross-section and when assembled the toy is in the form of a regular or an irregular solid. Fixation is performed by one single screw passing through bores in the connecting elements. In such a manner the toy elements forming the lateral faces of the spatial logical toy can be rotated along the spatial axes and by yielding several variation possibilities the toy is well suitable for stimulating logical thinking activity.

7 Claims, 12 Drawing Figures

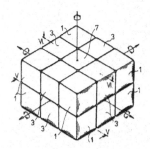

United States Patent [19]
Kuhn   [11] 4,169,336
                         [45] Oct. 2, 1979

[54] STRETCHABLE FIGURE EXHIBITING SLOW RECOVERY

[56] References Cited

June 26, 1956   J. BRUNOT ET AL   2,752,158
GAME APPARATUS
Filed Oct. 28, 1954

INVENTORS
James Brunot and Helen Brunot
BY Waters, Cole, Grindle & Watson
ATTORNEY

Popular Characters

Jan. 3, 1950 R. Y. ALLEN ET AL Des. 156,687
PUPPET
Filed June 4, 1949

April 5, 1932. L. L. JENNINGS Des. 86,676
DOLL
Filed Dec. 28, 1931

Dec. 16, 1930. W. E. DISNEY Des. 82,802
TOY OR SIMILAR ARTICLE
Filed Oct. 30. 1929

Oct. 11, 1966 S. F. SPEERS ET AL 3,277,602
TOY FIGURE HAVING MOVABLE JOINTS
Filed June 15, 1964 2 Sheets-Sheet 1

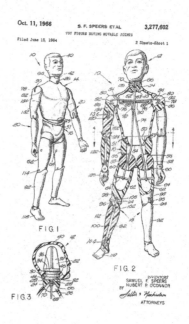

Iconic Sports Products

May 8, 1928.   1,668,969

J. E. MAYNARD

BASEBALL

Filed July 6, 1927

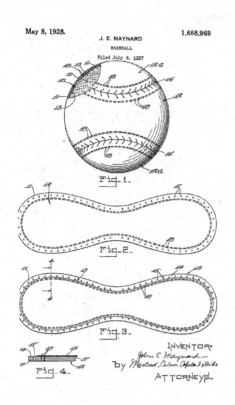

June 25, 1929.   G. L. PIERCE   1,718,305

BASKET BALL

Filed March 5, 1928

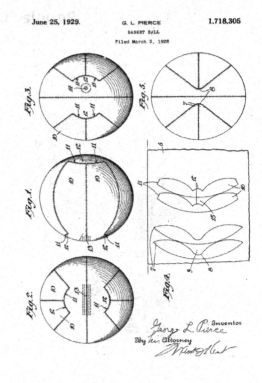

Oct. 27, 1925.   1,559,117

J. E. MAYNARD

FOOTBALL

Filed Oct. 11, 1923

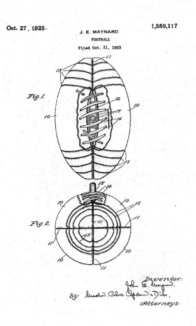

No. 878,254.   W. TAYLOR.   PATENTED FEB. 4, 1908.

GOLF BALL.

APPLICATION FILED SEPT. 11, 1906.

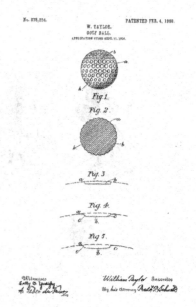

Star Wars Products

United States Patent [19]
McQuarrie et al.

[11] **Des. 251,627**
[45] ** Apr. 17, 1979

[54] **ROBOT**

[75] Inventors: Ralph McQuarrie, Los Angeles, Calif.; Norman Reynolds, St. Albans, England

[73] Assignee: Twentieth Century-Fox Film Corporation

[**] Term: 14 Years

[21] Appl. No.: 832,519

[22] Filed: Sep. 12, 1977

[51] Int. Cl. .... D21—01
[52] U.S. Cl. D21/150; D21/171
[58] Field of Search .... D34/15 AD, 4 R; 46/161

[56] **References Cited**
U.S. PATENT DOCUMENTS

D. 122,916 10/1940 Burkitt .... D34/15 AD
D. 197,288 1/1964 Campbell .... D34/15 AD
3,010,223 11/1961 Alderson 46/161

Primary Examiner—Melvin B. Feifer
Attorney, Agent, or Firm—Michael A. Painter

[57] **CLAIM**

The ornamental design for a robot, substantially as shown.

DESCRIPTION

FIG. 1 is a front elevation view of a robot showing our new design;
FIG. 2 is a side elevation view of the robot shown in FIG. 1; and
FIG. 3 is a rear elevation view of the robot shown in FIG. 1.

United States Patent [19]
Lucas, Jr. et al.

[11] **Des. 266,777**
[45] ** Nov. 2, 1982

[54] **TOY VEHICLE**

[75] Inventors: George W. Lucas, Jr., San Anselmo; Joseph E. Johnston, Fairfax, both of Calif.

[73] Assignee: Lucasfilm, Ltd., San Rafael, Calif.

[**] Term: 14 Years

[21] Appl. No.: 231,674

[22] Filed: Feb. 5, 1981

[51] Int. Cl. .... D21—01
[52] U.S. Cl. D21/134; D21/59;
D21/87; D21/148
[58] Field of Search .... D21/124, 128, 132, 134, D21/135–137, 140, 165, 148, 76, 78, 74, 59, 87; 46//1 R, 1 B, 115, 118

[56] **References Cited**
U.S. PATENT DOCUMENTS

2,482,334 9/1949 Fernald D21/74

OTHER PUBLICATIONS

Daiya Catalogue '80, p. 5, #730, B/O Gantry Crane. Wards Xmas Catalog, 1978, p. 361, Item "P" Acroyear.

Primary Examiner—Charles A. Rademaker
Attorney, Agent, or Firm—Townsend and Townsend

[57] **CLAIM**

The ornamental design for a toy vehicle, substantially as shown and described.

DESCRIPTION

FIG. 1 is a front perspective view of a toy vehicle showing my new design;
FIG. 2 is a right side perspective view thereof;
FIG. 3 is a left side perspective view thereof;
FIG. 4 is a rear perspective view thereof;
FIG. 5 is a right side perspective view of a modified form of the design shown in FIGS. 1 through 4;
FIG. 6 is a top plan view thereof;
FIG. 7 is a rear elevational view thereof;
FIG. 8 is a front elevational view thereof; and,
FIG. 9 is a bottom plan view thereof.

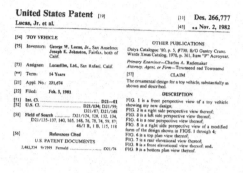

United States Patent [19]
Lucas, Jr. et al.

[11] **Des. 265,754**
[45] ** Aug. 10, 1982

[54] **TOY FIGURE**

[75] Inventors: George W. Lucas, Jr., San Anselmo; Ralph McQuarrie, Berkeley; Joseph E. Johnston, all of Calif.; Stuart Freeborn, Esher, England

[73] Assignee: Lucasfilm, Ltd., San Rafael, Calif.

[**] Term: 14 Years

[21] Appl. No.: 141,597

[22] Filed: Apr. 18, 1980

[51] Int. Cl. .... D21—01
[52] U.S. Cl. D21/180; D21/171;
D21/186
[58] Field of Search D21/180, 177, 166, 171, D21/186; D11/160

[56] **References Cited**
U.S. PATENT DOCUMENTS

D. 164,463 9/1951 White D21/186

OTHER PUBLICATIONS

Sears 1978 Xmas Book, p. 574, Illustration No. 13, left figure, Jawa.

Primary Examiner—Melvin B. Feifer
Attorney, Agent, or Firm—Townsend and Townsend

[57] **CLAIM**

The ornamental design for a toy figure, substantially as shown.

DESCRIPTION

FIG. 1 is a perspective front view of a toy figure illustrating the new design;
FIG. 2 is a perspective rear view thereof;
FIG. 3 is a front elevational view thereof;
FIG. 4 is a left side elevational view thereof;
FIG. 5 is a right side elevational view thereof;
FIG. 6 is a rear elevational view thereof;
FIG. 7 is a top plan view thereof;
FIG. 8 is a bottom view thereof.

United States Patent [19]
McQuarrie et al.

[11] **Des. 251,628**
[45] ** Apr. 17, 1979

[54] **ROBOT**

[75] Inventors: Ralph McQuarrie, Los Angeles, Calif.; John Stears, Gerrards Cross, England

[73] Assignee: Twentieth Century-Fox Film Corporation

[**] Term: 14 Years

[21] Appl. No.: 832,520

[22] Filed: Sep. 12, 1977

[51] Int. Cl. .... D21—01
[52] U.S. Cl. D21/150; D21/166
[58] Field of Search .... D34/15 AD, 4 R; 46/149, 46/113, 116, 119, 120

[56] **References Cited**
U.S. PATENT DOCUMENTS

D. 196,443 10/1963 Irwin .... D34/15 AD

OTHER PUBLICATIONS

Playthings, Mar., 1962, p. 363, upper right, "Mr. Atomic."

Primary Examiner—Melvin B. Feifer
Attorney, Agent, or Firm—Michael A. Painter

[57] **CLAIM**

The ornamental design for a robot, substantially as shown.

DESCRIPTION

FIG. 1 is a front perspective view of a robot showing our new design; and
FIG. 2 is a rear elevation view of the robot shown in FIG. 1.

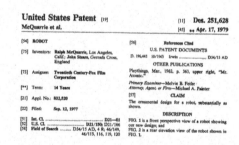

XV. Bits & Pieces

Adam Berg on Forming Friendships in Licensing

Adam Berg, Legendary Licensing Sales & New Business Development Exec., offers the following advice:

The licensing industry is to forming friendships under unusual circumstances what a maelstrom of cosmic dust is to forming stars; you never know what is going to happen, or why – but the result is something that is going to last a long, long time when it does.

It is as if Carl Sagan met Dale Carnegie, and while my story happened many decades ago, I remember it like yesterday and it still shines in my memory as bright as a newborn sun.

I had gotten to know a Vice President of Licensing at a company I had done business with, was currently doing business with, and knew I would be doing business with again. We got along. And after all the talk about deals, deal structures, and the usual back-and-forth about business, there was always time to talk about other things, and a friendship developed.

So, it was time for lunch. I eat anything. Still do. Always been that way. My parents were culinary nomads, and I never knew what I was going to be eating. At my house, it was eat it or don't eat it, but this is what we're eating today. One day Madagascar, the next day Texas; go figure.

I will also eat anything in copious amounts. Anyone who has been on the road with me in Las Vegas knows I favor the buffets. The bigger the better. I have been to all-you-can-eat Japanese sushi establishments and devoured several plates of sushi and sashimi stacked up like Aztec temples.

"Where should we go?" my friend pondered. Wrong question. I know all the buffets in Manhattan. "I know just the place!" I answered. We made the date and went to lunch.

I ate a normal buffet lunch for me. Not a hasty shovel-it-in-as-fast-as-you-can sprint, but a steady intake of various goodies in a calm, measured, and deliberate manner as I did not want to alarm the guy. Think of more a conveyor belt technique. My friend seemed to enjoy the food. We ate, we talked, we left.

The next day I got a phone call. He said, "Are you OK?" I said, "Yes, why?" He said "I was so sick after our lunch. I got home I was sick, I was sick all night, I barely made it to work." I said I was sorry to hear that. "Sorry? You are sorry? That food nearly killed me. What were you thinking?" I answered "I don't know. I eat there from time to time and never had a problem."

He must have been really sick because he has never forgotten that lunch. Whenever he passes a by a buffet in his travels, he goes and takes a picture of it and sends it to me from his phone. We have been friends ever since and laugh about it every time we speak.

You never know, so eat!

Sister Cathy Meets LJN President

Cathy Rondeau was one of the most prolific game inventors during the 1980s and 1990s, creating, among other games, GIRL TALK and DWEEBS GEEKS & WEIRDOS for Western Publishing and, ultimately, Hasbro. A naturally creative person, she would take her creativity to the next level when it came to making presentations to toy companies. While most toy company gatekeepers profess that they have an open-door policy to inventors and designers, the fact is that they are very possessive of their time and, as such, getting an appointment with them to show a new toy or game concept can be very challenging.

The story goes that Cathy had a new concept that she thought would be a perfect product for LJN Toys which was run by Jack Friedman. Her efforts at getting an appointment with Mr. Friedman proved unsuccessful but, undeterred, she was intent on making the presentation. So much so that she dressed up as a Catholic Nun and appeared at the LJN headquarters and told the receptionist that Sister Cathy was here to see Mr. Friedman. Who could refuse meeting with a Nun, right?

Long story short, he met with Sister Cathy and blessed the concept.

Reflections by Steve Herman

When Steve Herman was at Hearst he would always go to Cannes and it would always rain. Every time. One year, Hearst was going to Cannes to promote a Billy Zane movie for Phantom. Steve came up with the idea of giving away umbrellas with Phantom on them as a promotional item. As luck would have it— bad luck that is—it did not rain for the 3 days of the show that year.

****

In 1984, Steve met with one of the partners of a small start-up company, Comic Images. They were created to exploit the newly defined direct market; the result of Marvel and DC recognizing that they could not only pump out comic books, but they could also sell licensed merchandise in the growing number of comic book/fantasy stores. However, since both companies had already exclusively licensed most product categories for wholesale/retail distribution, they decided the comic bookstores were a new and distinct channel. The challenge of this channel of distribution is that you are selling to a fan base through thousands of small independent shops with limited space and capital. The one-year license that Comic Images held for three Superhero characters for t-shirts worked spectacularly well for the first three months, but then the store owners wanted either more t's with different characters or the same characters on a different product.

The solution: Comic Images would license three Superhero characters, for three product categories, for one year for the direct market only. However, when sales for one of those products started to fall off, Comic Images could surrender that product and produce a new product, thus keeping their product mix fresh.

****

Steve also recalls two stories from his days with the YOUNG ASTRONAUTS program, i.e., the only licensing program that could not fail!

In late 1984 or early 1985, while working at Marvel Comics, he was asked to attend a meeting with their sister company, Curtis Circulation, one of the largest distributors of magazines to newsstands nationally. The purpose of the meeting was to hear a proposal for a new science magazine for kids. At that meeting, Steve learned that since President Reagan had cut Federal spending on education, he had been lambasted by nationally syndicated columnist Jack Anderson. As a result, the President founded and chaired a commission that included Jack Anderson and Hugh Downs to revitalize the math and science curriculum nationwide and decided to fund these changes from the private sector. The commission's idea was to tie math and science lessons to the monthly space shuttle launches.

They asked Steve whether he thought that James Industries, the owner and manufacturer of the SLINKY toy, would pay $5000.00 for the exposure of an astronaut using a SLINKY to demonstrate wave theory in a live television broadcast from the space shuttle.

Recognizing the licensing potential, Steve suggested retaining a graphic designer to develop a strong logo and color story and then, based on the exposure of the new magazine, an animated TV show which Marvel Studios would develop. With strong promotional partners, they could launch a licensing program that would generate a continuous income stream to fund their new educational programs.

Within 6 months, he was able to license the promotional rights to MCDONALDS for fast food, QUAKER for a CAPT'N CRUNCH promotion, PEPSI for cola, and GENERAL FOODS for food products. The promotional partners were impressive as well. CBS licensed the TV show, activewear was licensed to ADIDAS, toys to COLECO, plus 15 other top-notch product licensees. With a new magazine, a new TV show and the ad spending and marketing clout of big-name promotional partners to support the blue-chip product licensees, everyone felt that "We Could Not Fail". That is, until the Challenger exploded 73 seconds into its January 1986 flight.

The second story was from late 1985. Steve, his staff, and about 20 of the YOUNG ASTRONAUTS licensees were invited to a private reception at the White House to meet President Reagan and celebrate the official launch of the licensing program. In attendance were the CEO's of GENERAL FOODS, MCDONALD'S, PEPSI, QUAKER OATS, ADIDAS, COLECO, etc.

Upon arrival, the group gathered in a waiting room and were addressed by the Secretary of Protocol who advised them of what was to take place. He explained certain rules that must be followed, including the fact that no one should ever hand anything to the President. If anyone wanted to give something to him, it was to be given to the Secret Service agent who would make sure the President got it. Considering that someone had recently tried to shoot the President, the Secret Service was exceptionally diligent.

The President and Nancy Reagan entered the room. The group formed a line to meet the President and First Lady. Everything was going splendidly until the CEO

of COLECO decided that the rules didn't apply to him, and he tried to hand President Reagan a CABBAGE PATCH DOLL dressed as an astronaut. He never even fully extended his arm before two Secret Service agents threw him to the floor, handcuffed him, and escorted him from the room without his feet ever touching the floor. As they carried him out, he turned toward Steve and yelled, "Steve, do something!" Other than watching him carried from the Oval Office, there wasn't much that he could do.

Super Licensing Salesman

Greg Battersby recalls a story from his G+W days working for a division called H. Koch & Sons which made ejection systems and harnesses for Navy pilots. He was asked to review a license proposal involving a patent owned by another company that could be used in conjunction with the Koch system to potentially solve a serious problem.

The problem was a simple, but technically complex, problem. When a Navy pilot ejected or bailed out from a plane over the ocean, the pilot would frequently land in the water. At that point, the parachute would quickly fill with water and potentially drag the pilot under. If the pilot was conscious, he or she could manually release the parachute and the problem would be averted. If, however, the pilot was unconscious at the point of impact, the pillow would be unable to release the parachute and would be dragged under to meet an untimely death. Unfortunately, that occurred in many instances, since the pilot was being violently ejected from a plane traveling hundreds of miles per hour, thousands of feet above the water.

The objective was to come up with an automatic switch that would release the parachute from the harness in the presence of water. In theory, the problem appeared to be easily solvable, i.e., provide a release mechanism that would automatically disengage the parachute in the presence of water. What made the obvious solution potentially problematic was the possibility that a pilot may eject in a rainstorm which, by its very nature, meant that switch would be exposed to water and, if triggered, would release the parachute high above the ocean, thus potentially ruining the pilot's whole day.

In any event, a third-party company came up with a neat product that would potentially solve the problem and overcome the obvious obstacles. They had obtained a patent for their switch and offered to license it to Koch.

Greg was asked to contact them and try to negotiate a favorable license agreement, which he did, contacting the company's attorney and setting up a meeting. At the meeting, the attorney told Greg that his client was looking for a high six figure advance against a double-digit royalty. While Greg thought that the ask was outrageously high considering the margins in government contracting coupled with the size of the market, he felt obligated to take it back to the client, and he did.

The client's response was curious. He said that the advance and royalty being sought would effectively triple the cost of their product, making it commercially impossible to sell to the Navy since they were working under a fixed fee contract. He asked Greg, however, to tell the attorney that Koch would be interested in learning whether he was able to sell that license to any other party.

Greg thought that the response was curious, so he asked the Koch president whether he was asking for a "right of first refusal" provision. The president replied, "Hell, no. If he can sell that deal to anybody, I want to hire him as head of our sales department, because he must be a great salesman."

Michael Jonas—So You Want to Be a Millionaire?

In the early 90s, a friend and business colleague came to Michael Jonas, a principle at a game company called Time for Two, with a game idea and a "title" and asked if he would create a multi-player family game. It was outside the bailiwick of the company who, at the time, had only been creating games for couples (romance and relationships.)

Though Time for Two was not interested in the gameplay and structure as it was proposed, they were excited and saw the potential in keeping the title, "You Just Became a Millionaire." As such, they created the game and began selling it and it was very well received.

Fast forward: Disney/ABC launched the TV show, "Who Wants to Be a Millionaire?" and they introduced a board game with the same title.

Michael contacted their attorney, Greg Battersby, who was in regular touch with Hasbro, knew they were interested in licensing their game, and understood that Jonas' company had a superior trademark such that Disney/ABC could not register their game's name.

Hasbro wanted to move quickly to take advantage of the popularity of the TV show and "money." They were so anxious to get it out to their stores that Time for Two shipped the production film to them BEFORE they had finalized a license agreement ... it was all done on Greg's word that Hasbro's attorneys were honorable people. It turned out they and Hasbro were.

Michael is sure that Hasbro still is, but the world we live and work in now has certainly changed — strong licensing agreements, particularly in the digital age, are even more important than they were then.

Spencer Rosenheck—Full Chinese Escort

Spencer Rosenheck of Pacific Bridge Group, LLC recalls being contracted by the Iconix Brand Group to expand its licensing efforts into Asia Pacific back in 2005. One of its portfolio brands was LONDON FOG. After several bazaar months traveling around mainland China trying to drum up interest, he had finally gotten some traction with several of the brands in several countries. LONDON FOG had some interested parties.

His last hurdle was a licensee who was a holdover from the previous IP owner. This licensee had become a pirate and no other manufacturer/retailer in China would touch the property unit this party was dealt with. The licensee was based in a very northern city of Harbin along the border with Russia. Spencer had spoken with the owner of the "operation" who demanded that Spencer come and see him in Harbin. He wanted to renew a legitimate license with Iconix so he could expand from his current seven stores in the city of Harbin. In Spencer's mind, this would be like giving a small retailer based in Anchorage, Alaska the license for all the USA.

Nevertheless, Spencer felt that he had to go and "deal" with him. The US State Department at the time had issued a firm warning to US businesspeople advising against traveling to outer Chinese provinces to settle disputes. The practice of detaining foreign businesspeople to gain favorable negotiating terms had become somewhat common. The CEO of Iconix kind of laughed it off and said have a nice trip. So, he left Shanghai on a Friday afternoon with his best Chinese pal, Jun. He took regular phone screenshots with his GPS coordinates and regularly texted them to his wife back in LA.

When he arrived in Harbin, he was greeted at 11 pm with a full uniformed Chinese military escort. Three old Cadillac limousines were adorned with Chinese flags on the corners of the hood of the car. It was a red army motorcade that was meant to intimidate, and it did. They took him to the main plaza in downtown Harbin, Stalin Square. The hotel and the entire city were built by the Russians before WWII.

Spencer's room was the entire top floor of this 10-story building. A dozen men piled out of the three cars and escorted Spencer and Jun to the room. It was now about midnight and the "welcoming party" spent the next three hours in his cavernous hotel apartment discussing the following days' negotiations with Spencer through his interpreter Jun.

Alcohol and women were regularly offered during the meeting, as well as pictures of the seven stores in which he would be touring the next day. Throughout the three-hour meeting, Spencer's host constantly referenced and reinforced their extensive governmental and military connections. Spencer was exhausted. They would not leave. Just after 3 a.m. they finally did. Then the phone rang, and he was asked, "Do you want a Russian girl?" "No, thank you." The phone rang again, "Do you want a Chinese girl, a Mongolian girl?" "No thanks."

The next two days were a farcical tour of the seven stores and the operational capabilities of the hosts. Spencer had managed his hosts' expectations of the trip and reinforced the sentiment that he was not able to grant the license for LONDON FOG to them. He was only an adviser. The second Spencer could leave without insulting them, he rushed to the airport. Back in Shanghai, he felt safe. Safe enough to tell his Harbin friends that New York had decided to go in another direction.

Best Deals Ever/Never Done by Jerry Kapner

-Best deal I ever made that I probably shouldn't have initially: A handshake deal with Ertl, who I knew from my days as a toy buyer, for a $5000 guarantee for a DUKES OF HAZARD die cast. Their first quarterly royalty check was for over $1 million, the largest quarterly royalty payment that Warner Bros. had ever received at that point in history.

-The best deal that I didn't make, that I wanted to: A private label for plus size apparel for Sears offered a 7-figure guarantee to OPRAH, just **before** we launched her nationally at King World. She declined the deal, with the rationale and prescience that she did not want to be identified as "plus-size", did not want to be overexposed, and she didn't shop at Sears (that's the only one that I can still argue in hindsight).

-Best FU to a winey licensee: A licensee for a Spielberg project called me up screaming about the "rules, regulations and secrecy" surrounding this particular property. I put the phone down on my desk, tore up some papers I had sitting there, and told the licensee that he didn't have a problem anymore, as I just tore up his contract. He called back to apologize and see if I could restore his rights.

-Best FU to a winey agent: A client offered to renew my representation by cutting my commission in half.

-Most obscene licensing-oriented proposal: A collectible firm called me up and wanted access to the bloodied shirt MONICA SELES was wearing when she was stabbed on a tennis court. Given my fiduciary role at IMG, I had to call her and her agent and present the offer. And they say that licensing folks have no shame.

Greg Battersby's Best Excuse by a Licensee for Not Paying Royalties

In the early years of his practice, Greg was representing a toy inventor who had licensed a property to one of the larger toy companies in New York City. The property was featured by that company at that year's Toy Fair, building out their showroom around the property.

When the time came for the toy company to pay the client its royalties, no check appeared. Greg was retained to pursue the matter with the toy company and set up a meeting to discuss it with their president.

The meeting was quite cordial but when Greg asked their president why he hadn't paid his client what they owed, he gave Greg perhaps the best excuse that he's ever heard, "I know that we have a contract with your client and that, under the contract, we are obligated to pay him royalties based on our sales of the products. I also know that we have sales and that under the contract, we owe them royalties." He paused. Greg then asked, "So why aren't you paying the royalties?" He sat there quietly, thought a bit, and then gave the best response Greg ever heard, "Because I don't like them." Greg was speechless.

Logic ultimately prevailed, however, and the client eventually received his royalty payment … late, without interest, of course.

Carole Francesca—Women in Licensing: We've Come a Long Way Baby

In 1982, I was a young, newly minted licensing manager at a movie studio in NYC. A colleague introduced me to Murray Altchuler, VP at LCA, the largest independent licensing agency at the time. Murray invited me to a meeting to discuss his idea of creating an association for licensors and agencies. While licensing is something that's been around since the 1920s, it was still a scattered business based around toys, kids' apparel, and tchotchkes. The idea of industry standards or any semblance of cohesiveness was still a foreign concept. Even the terms "marketing" and "strategic planning" didn't solidly enter the licensing vernacular until the introduction of STRAWBERRY SHORTCAKE in the mid-1980s.

On the day of the meeting, about 30 of us assembled in the conference room of Jim Henson's Muppet townhouse to kick off ideas about an association. My boss thought the idea was "dumb" but went with me to see what it was all about. As happens with every generation, most of the licensing veterans didn't see the need for any kind of association and liked things the way they were. The younger, newer people like myself loved the idea of trying to bring together a diverse group of companies and people together to network and share ideas. I mean, where's the downside in that? During the meeting, my boss leaned over to me and whispered, "don't get any ideas about volunteering for this thing." "Dude" (I said in my head, not out loud), "I'm jumping into this very cool new thing with both feet!"

Shortly after the meeting, the LIA (Licensing Industry Association) was born, and I was determined to elbow my way into its all-male board. I volunteered to become its secretary, a "girl position" because none of the guys wanted to take notes at the board meetings, type them up and send them out. It was one of the smartest moves I ever made and was the first step in my 20+ year "career" with the Association, capped off by my election as Chair of the Board in 2000. And – no small thing – I gained a dear friend and generous mentor in Murray Altchuler; a 30-year friendship that continued until he died in 2012.

Unlike the highly-organized industry it is today, with "how-to" books on royalty rates and a million articles covering advances, guarantees, and marketing, licensing deals back then seemed to be made on the fly, pulling numbers and royalty rates out of the air. And not everyone was willing to share information with newbies like me. The first deal I ever negotiated was for a major motion picture, and I had to find a licensee to make toy model space stations. While I had figured out basic guidelines to negotiate a deal, my boss basically told me to figure it out myself. I leafed through the Toy Fair directory, picked up the phone, and started calling companies, finally landing on a company who said "We're interested. What are the deal terms?" By the end of the conversation, I had closed my first, albeit not my finest, deal. Trying to do it without the right tools had made me feel stupid and uncertain. There had to be a better way to figure this out.

While the LIA was bringing people together, there was no path at the time to educate members about the ins and outs of licensing. This was especially impacting women in the industry, most of whom were left to feel their way along individually. Many were as frustrated as I was. I thought, "We're all having the same problems. Our bosses aren't helping. Let's figure this out together."

I pulled together a list of women I knew in licensing and invited them to meet at a colleague's Manhattan apartment. That first get-together was well attended, and the feedback was enthusiastic. After a few more meetings with great turnouts, it was apparent I was on to something and created Women in Licensing.

As it grew, Lois Sloane stepped up to help with new member outreach. We moved our meetings to member conference rooms, networked, brought in speakers, traded information about negotiating deals, attracting licensees and retailers, and how to further our careers. Many of us formed life-long friendships along the way, as we rose in the industry to become dynamic leaders heading up major licensing divisions.

Women in Licensing lasted for about five years until the demands of a new corporate job made it difficult to continue leading the group. Unbeknownst to me at the time, WIL had started a butterfly effect across parts of the industry. Members who worked in specific fields in licensing started up other "Women In _____" organizations within their own categories. One industry friend, Susan Matsumoto, co-founded Women in Toys, which later  absorbed WIL into its organization. I'm pleased that, over the decades, Women in Toys & Licensing has become a well-respected global organization with chapters in 25 countries that continues to help women advance their careers in the toy and licensing industries.

The licensing industry has grown tremendously since then, not only in size but in significance around the world. I will say though, it was a hell of a lot of fun growing up in the industry when it was all just beginning to gel together; when everyone was still figuring out how to use "marketing" and "licensing" together in a sentence and when the Licensing Show was just a few dozen tables at an NYC hotel. It's kinda like watching your kids grow up into real and serious adults. You love that part, but you still smile when you remember their first day at school.

XVI. The Lighter Side of Licensing

Garfield Comics

Peanuts Comics

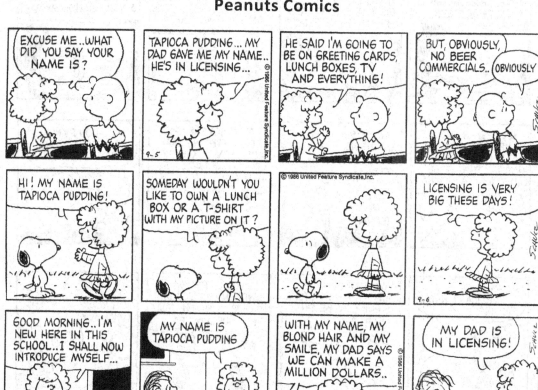

WHO ARE YOU, AND WHY ARE YOU WALKING WITH MY SWEET BABBOO?

I'M NOT HER SWEET BABBOO! MY NAME IS TAPIOCA PUDDING...

MY DAD IS IN LICENSING.. MY FACE IS GOING TO BE ON T-SHIRTS AND LUNCH BOXES..

IT'D LOOK A LOT BETTER ON A DOG DISH!

HI! MY NAME IS TAPIOCA PUDDING! I KNOW

MY DAD IS IN LICENSING..MY PICTURE IS GOING TO BE ON EVERY PRODUCT IN THE COUNTRY..

DO YOU THINK YOU AND I HAVE MUCH IN COMMON? I DON'T KNOW

DO YOU LIKE UP-FRONT MONEY?

THAT WAS A GOOD MOVIE..REBECCA'S MY FAVORITE ACTRESS..

I WONDER IF SHE'S INTO LICENSING... DID I TELL YOU THAT'S WHAT I'M GOING TO DO?

MY NAME WILL BE ON EVERY PRODUCT IN THE COUNTRY, AND........... AM I BORING YOU?

NO, I ALWAYS LIKE TO REST MY FACE IN A MARSHMALLOW SUNDAE!

YOU SEE, MY DAD'S NAME IS JOE PUDDING SO IT WAS ONLY NATURAL THAT I'D BE CALLED TAPIOCA PUDDING..

MY DAD'S IN LICENSING, YOU KNOW I KNOW

WITH MY NAME AND FACE ON EVERY GREETING CARD AND CEREAL BOX IN THE COUNTRY, MY DAD SAYS WE'LL MAKE A MILLION..

YOU DON'T KNOW ANYTHING ABOUT INVESTMENTS, DO YOU?

HI! MY NAME IS TAPIOCA PUDDING I KNOW

MY DAD IS IN LICENSING..MY PICTURE IS GOING TO BE ON GREETING CARDS AND LUNCH BOXES

IF YOU WERE MY BOYFRIEND, YOU WOULDN'T HAVE TO CARRY MY PICTURE IN YOUR WALLET..

IT WOULD ALREADY BE ON YOUR LUNCH BOX! I CAN'T STAND IT!

Archie Comics Strips

Other Comic Strips

THE PASSING OF A LICENSING AGENT

©1998 Wiley Miller / dist. by The Washington Post Writers Group   E-mail: wiley@wileytoons.com   Web Site: www.wileytoons.com

NON SEQUITUR
BY WILEY

Index

A

Abdul, Paula, 108

Advanstar, 50, 55

Allen, Paul, 41

Aloia, Tony, 39

Altchuler, Murray, vi, 12, 52, 54–55, 123–24, 145–46

AMERICAN GRAFITTI, 44–45

American Greetings, 8

Anderson, Jack, 139

Anheuser-Busch, 13, 104–5, 126

APOLLO CREED, 47, 48

Apple Computer, 41

Archie Comics, 30, 55, 151

ARM & HAMMER, 12

Ash, Francesca, v, 49

B

Bally Midway, 32–33

Barbera, Joe, 2

Barnaby, Howard, 121

BARNEY RUBBLE, 2

Basic Fun, 95, 110, 119-121

BATMAN, 12, 17, 25

Battersby, Greg, 34, 121, 126, 41, 144

BEACH BOYS, 23

Beanstalk, 54

BEATLES, 26

Bell, Jim, 83

Benton, Jim, 39

Berg, Adam, v, 137

BEWITCHED, 37

BIG BIRD, 90

Blackman, Marty, vi, 99-101

BLUES BROTHERS, 50–51

Boise State University, 126

Borden, Lester, 9, 55

Borden Ink, 109-110

Boucher, Connie, 26

Bowling, Mike, v, 92

Braddock, Benjamin, 49

Brady, Tom, 125

BRATZ, 50, 77–78

BRITNEY SPEARS, 107

BROOKS BROTHERS, 4

BRUCE LEE, 37

Bryant, Carter, 77

BUD LIGHT, 101

BUFFALO BOB SMITH, 32

Buffer, Michael, 127126

BUGS BUNNY, 15, 18–20

BURGER TIME, 34

BUSTER, 25

C

Caan, James, 47

CABBAGE PATCH KIDS, 27–29, 99, 108, 121, 140

CAPT'N CRUNCH, 140

Cardi B, 126

CARDIN, 8

Carnegie, Dale, 137

Carney, Art, 2

Caron, Louise, v, 52-54,123

CBS, 26, 38, 140

CELINE DION, 37

CHARLES BARKLEY, 17

CHARMING BILLY, 49

CHIEF THUNDERTHUD, 32

CHRIS PAUL, 20

CHRISTOPHER ROBIN, 80

Clark, Dick, 103

Coca-Cola, 13, 100

Coleco, 27–28, 48, 140

Colgate-Palmolive, 123

Columbia, 1, 3, 6, 10

Cooney, Joan Ganz, 92

Connie Van Epps, 113

COTTON, 13

Criss, Peter, 109

Cruise, Tom, 37

D

DALLAS COWBOYS, 101

DAMIAN LILLARD, 20

Dangerfield, Rodney, 103-104

Davis, Anthony, 20

DAVY CROCKETT, 25

DELAURENTIS, 3

Descente, 23–24

DISCOVERY, 73, 78, 81, 85

Disney, 25–26, 44, 46, 79–82

DOCTOR DOLITTLE, 45

DOLL BABIES, 27

DOMINO, 34

DONALD DUCK, 80

Dorfman, Alan, v, 119

DOWNTON ABBEY, 39

DR-DOS, 43

Dubren, Ron, 89–91

DWARFS, 25, 49

DWEEBS GEEKS & WEIRDOS, 138

E

Ebert, Roger, 17

Eckert, Robert, 79

Edgar Rice Burroughs, 44

EEYORE, 80

ELMO, 89–92

EMPIRE STRIKES BACK, 45

ESPN, 114

EXPENDABLES, 48

Expocon, 55

F

FAO Schwarz, 113

FARRAH FAWCETT, 5

Favata, Fred, 55

Feldman, Allan, v, 10

Ferdinand, Jed, iv

Fisher-Price, 92

Flaherty, Stephen, 48

FLINTSTONES, 2,9

FORD, 94

Foreman, Jay, v, 107

Francesca, Carole, 145

Friedman, Jack, 138

Friedman, Neil, 89, 91

Fueller, Simon, 107

Furano, Dell, v, 109

G

G+W, 34, 121, 140

GALAXIAN, 32–33

GAMBLER, 104

GARBAGE PAIL KIDS, 29

GARFIELD, 149

GATORADE, 19

GEORGIA PACIFIC, 13

Georgopolis, Mike, 26

GIRLS CLUBS, 108

GODFATHER, 37

Gotti, John, 91

GRACE KELLY, 38

Greene, Joe, 100

Grimes, Chuck, 121

Grimes & Battersby, 121, 164

GUND, 40

H

Hakan, Brian, v, 104

Hallmark, 8, 12, 106

Hammill, Dorothy, 13

Hanna-Barbera, 2

HARE JORDAN, 17–18

HARLEY DAVIDSON, 126

HARRY POTTER, 17

Hearst, 55, 138

HEINEKEN, 13

HEPBURN, AUDREY, 37

Herman, Steve, v, 55, 138

HERSHEY, 14

Hilton, Paris, 125

HONEYMOONERS, 2

HOPALONG CASSIDY, 25

Hosmer, Bruce, 121

Houle, Michelle, vi

HOWDY DOODY, 1, 3, 25, 32

HUCKLEBERRY HOUND, 2, 6, 9

I

IBM, 41–44

IBM PC, 42–43

Iconix, 143

Ideal Toys, 2, 93

Ita Golzman, 38

J

JACKIE CHAN, 20

Jackson, Michael, 37, 80

Jakks Pacific, 28, 83

JAMES BOND movies, 12-13

JAMES DEAN, 35–37

James, LeBron, 20, 125

Jarocki, Stan, vi, 32-33

Jefferds, Vince, 81

JEFF GORDON, 20

JELLYSTONE PARK, 9

Jenner, Kylie, 126

JOHNNY JUPITER, 9

Jonas, Michael, 142

JORDAN, 17–20, 118

JUSTIN, ED vi, 1–9, 26

K

Kalle Torma, v, 124

Kamen, Kay, 25

KANGA, 80

Kapner, Jerry, v, 144

Kayser Roth Hosiery, 34,121

Kenny Rogers, 104-107

Kildall, Gary, 41-42

King, Nancy, 106

KISS, 109-111

Kosinski, Chief Judge Alex, 78

L

Ladd, Alan, 44

Landry, Tom, 99

Larian, Isaac, 77

Larkins, Ted, v, 35

LaRocca, Sal, 114

Laswell, Shirley Slesinger, 80

Lauer, Dan, v, 97

Lawrence, Andrew, 122

LeBron James, 20, 125

Lee, Spike, 18

Leifer, Bernie, 50

LIMA, 52, 54, 55, 114-116, 123-124, 164

LITE BEER, 99

LITTLE HOUSE, 5

LITTLE PEOPLE, 27

LITTLE PIGS, 25

LMA, 55

LMCA, 10–12

LONDON FOG, 142

LOONEY TUNES, 17- 20, 90,116

Lucas, George, 44

M

MACY'S, 38,104

Madden, John, 99

Major Ugly, 54

MARIAH CAREY, 37

Mark Freedman, 30

Martin, Billy, 99

Marvel Comics, 109, 139

Marvel/KISS, 109-111

Mattel, 28, 77–79, 92

MAVERICK, 25

McCann, John, v, 120

MCDONALD'S, 140

MENSA, 11-12

MGA, 77–79

MICHAEL JORDAN, 17–20

MICHIGAN J FROG, 118

MICKEY MOUSE, 25

Microsoft, 41–44

Miller, Nicole, 113

MINNIE MOUSE, 80

Mirage Studios, 29–30

MONKEES, 3

MONT BLANC, 58

MORK & MINDY, 121

Motown, 117

MS-DOS, 43, 44

MTA, 57-58

MUGGSY BOGUES, 17

Murray, Bill, 19

Murtha, Gene, 90

N

NATIONAL FOOTBALL PLAYERS
    ASSOCIATION, 14

NATIONAL HOCKEY LEAGUE,
13

NBA, 19, 101, 107, 113-116

NBC, 1, 6, 9–10, 116, 128

NCAA, 23–24

NEW BALANCE, 37

New York Toy Fair, 91

NFL, 99-101

NIKE, 17, 105

NINJA TURTLES, 29–31

Nordic licensing, 122

O

O'Donnell, Rosie, 91

Ohio State University, 126

Olympics, 24

O'Melveny & Myers, 78

O'Neill, Ryan, 47

OPRAH, 144

OREO cookies, 12

OSH KOSH, 50

OZ, 38

P

Pacific Bridge Group, 142

PAC-MAN, 32–33

Palin, Sarah, 125

Paramount Pictures, 36, 121, 164

Parker Brothers, 28, 96

Paterson, Tim, 43

PATRICK EWING, 17

PEANUTS, 7, 26, 149

PEBBLES, 2,8

Penn State, 11

PEPSI, 36–37, 140

PEZ, 31

PFIZER, 12

PIGLET, 80

Pilgrim Products, 55

PINK COOKIE, 39

PINK PANTHER, 37

PIXIE, 6

Playmates Toys, 30, 97, 98

PLUTO, 80

POKEMON, 50, 119

POLLYANNA THE PIG, 10

POOH, 74, 79-85

Postal, Carole, v, 38, 48

Postal, Robert, 38

POUND PUPPIES, 50, 92–95

POWER RANGERS, 50, 120

PRODIGYWORKS, 11-12

Q

Quackenbush, Mike, v, 71

QUAKER OATS, 140

R

RACE JAM, 20

Ralston-Purina, 31

RAMBO, 48

RAWLINGS, 105-6

Reagan, Nancy, 140

Reagan, Ronald, 87, 139–40

Regan, Maura, 122

Reitman, Ivan, 18

Revoyr, Jack, vi, 20–24

Reynolds, Burt, 47

Richards, Tim, 105

RIN TIN TIN, 5

Riotto, Charles, iv, 50, 115, 124

Riswold, Jim, 17

Roberts, Xavier, 26–27, 29, 108

ROCKY, 46-48

Rogers, Kenny, 104-107

Romanelli, Dan, 17

ROMAN HOLIDAY, 37

Rondeau, Cathy, 138

Roney, Nell, v, 101

Rosenheck, Spencer, v, 142

ROVER DANGERFIELD, 103

Russell, Bill, 105

S

Saban Entertainment, 30

SABRINA, 37

Sagan, Carl, 137

Sallis, Richard, 98

SATURDAY NIGHT FEVER, 4-5

Scanlan, Arlene, v, 57, 103

Schlaifer, Roger, 27

Schlaifer-Nance, 27-28

Schlitz, Don, 105

Schnaid, Charles, v, 73

Schneider, Burt, 6

Scholastic, 55

Schwartz, Tara, 116

SCOOBY DOO, 17

SCRABBLE, 95

Sega, 48,121

Selchow & Righter, 96

SESAME STREET, 89-92

SEVEN-UP, 100

SG Companies, 50

Shenker, Stanley, 83

Shire, Talia, 47

Siegel, Seth, 54

Simmons, Gene, 109, 126

Simon, Danny, v, 38, 51

Simon & Schuster, 170

SIMPSONS, 38

SLINKY, 139

Sloane, Lois, 146

SmackDown, 83

Smith, Pete, 25

Snodgress, Carrie, 47

SNOOPY, 9, 26

SNUGGLE, 13

SOLAR FOX, 34

SPACE INVADERS, 32–33

SPACE JAM, 20, 22-24

SPALDING, 105

SPIDER-MAN, 37

Spitz, Karen, 38

SPUDETTES, 101

SPUDS MACKENZIE, 101–3

SPY JAM, 20

Stanley, Paul, 109

STAR TREK, 31,38,121

STAR WARS, 7, 31, 44–46,135

STEELERS, 100

Steiner, Bob, 93

Stern, David, 114

STETSON, 13

Stone, Allan, 12

Stone, Martin, 1

Strand, Robert, v, 113

Strauss, Levi, 24

STRAWBERRY SHORTCAKE, 7, 145

SUPER BOWL, 17–18, 101-03, 125

SUPERMAN, 14, 17

SUPER SOAKER, 119-120

Swarovski crystal, 116

Swift, Taylor, 125

Syracuse University, 126

T

TASMANIAN DEVIL, 90

TEDDY RUXPIN doll, 90

Ted Larkins' book, 35

TEENAGE MUTANT NINJA TURTLES, 29-31, 98

TELETUBBIES, 50

TICKLE ME ELMO, 89-92

TIFFANY'S, 36

TIGGER, 80

TIMBERLAND, 58

Time Warner, 123

Tonka, 94

TONY HAWK, 20

TOP GUN, 37

Torma, Kalle v, 122

Toss, Linda, 115

Total Licensing, 170

TRIVIAL PURSUIT, 95–96

TURTLES, 29–31

TWEETY, 90

TWIGGY, 26

Tyco, 89–92

U

UCLA, 20–24

United Artists, 44, 47

University of California, 21

University of Texas, 126

V

Viacom, 170

W

WAGON TRAIN, 25

Walt Disney Company, 79,80

Warner Brothers, 13,17

Warner Communications, 13, 123–25

WATERBABIES, 98

Weathers, Carl, 47

Wepner, Chuck, 47

Western Publishing, 138

WHASSUP, 126

Wicked Cool Toys, 28

WILSON, 105

WINNIE-THE-POOH, 74, 79-82

World Wrestling Entertainment,
    83-84

Wurstlin, Michael, 95

X

Xerox, 41

Y

YOGI BEAR, 2,6,8-9

Yoshida, 35–37

YOUNG ASTRONAUTS, 139-140

YU GI OH, 119

Z

Zane, Billy, 138

Zilli, Jonathan, 36

Zoe, Rachel, 125

ZORRO, 37

Amazon's Top Licensing Book

The most complete licensing book ever written, covering:

- Licensing categories and the licensing process
- A history of successful properties, unique products and key people
- Point-by-point analysis of licensing agreements
- Topics include:
- Buying & selling licensed products
- Protection
- Administration
- Key worldwide licensing markets
- Electronic Link to collection of contracts and forms

All for $39.95 for paperback; $32.95 for Kindle Version

"Finally, a straight forward road map addressing all the critical stages and considerations involved with executing a successful licensing program. The book is an indispensable resource for anyone who wants to successfully navigate through the licensing industry." Charles M. Riotto, President emeritus, LIMA

"This book addresses an industry need for relevant information and instruction in a manner that serves both the novice and the expert. The comprehensive collection of materials from such an impressive group of industry experts is unparalleled." Rick VanBrimmer, Past Chairman, LIMA

To Purchase: Visit Kent's website at www.thebusinessoflicensing.com
or Amazon at www.amazon.com

168

BROWNE, GORDON, & VAN RAALTE, LLC.

> ➤ BROWNE, GORDON & VAN RAALTE, LLC. (BG&VR) IS A MANAGEMENT CONSULTING COMPANY FOR CONSUMER PRODUCTS COMPANIES THAT PROVIDES BUSINESS DEVELOPMENT, LINE PLANNING, LICENSING INFORMATION, AND INDUSTRY ANALYSIS. WE GUIDE YOU ON HOW TO UTILIZE LICENSING AS AN ADDED-VALUE MARKETING TOOL FOR YOUR BUSINESS.

> ➤ WE OFFER DIRECTION AND EXPERTISE TO PROPERTY OWNERS, LICENSING AGENCIES, AND MANUFACTURERS ON BEST PRACTICES, DEVELOPMENT, AND POSITIONING.

> ➤ WHAT SETS BG&VR APART IS THE THREE FOUNDERS' VARIED EXPERIENCE IN THE INDUSTRY. WE HAVE OWNED OUR OWN COMPANIES, MANAGED LICENSING DEPARTMENTS FOR MAJOR BRANDS, ACQUIRED LICENSES, SOURCED, AND MANUFACTURED AND SOLD LICENSED PRODUCT TO ALL RETAIL CHANNELS DURING OUR COLLECTIVE 100 PLUS YEARS OF INDUSTRY SUCCESS.

WE CAN HELP YOU...

CONTACT US:

C. WOODROW "WOODY" BROWNE / ALAN GORDON / PETER VAN RAALTE

WWW.BGVRLLC.COM

About the Author

Greg Battersby is the managing member of The Battersby Law Group, LLC, a Westport, CT based intellectual property law firm. He has almost 50 years of experience in patents, trademarks, and licensing law. Before founding Battersby Law Group, he had been a founding partner in Grimes & Battersby after having been previously associated with two major New York City IP law firms and serving as senior counsel at Gulf + Western Industries (now Viacom) which owned Paramount Pictures, Madison Square Garden and Simon & Schuster.

Greg has an A.B. degree from Seton Hall University and a law degree from Fordham Law School where he was an editor of Fordham's *Urban Law Journal*. He worked his way through law school, working in the advanced development section of the quality control laboratory at Grumman Aerospace on NASA's Lunar Excursion Module ("LEM") and the Navy's F-14 projects. Greg is admitted to practice before the New York and Connecticut bars and as a patent attorney before the USPTO.

He served as the General Counsel for the International Licensing Industry Merchandisers' Association ("LIMA") from 1996 through 2019 and was a member of its Executive Committee. He was inducted into LIMA's Licensing Hall of Fame in 2009—the only practicing attorney ever to be so inducted. He has also been an officer and member of the Board of Directors of the New York Intellectual Property Law Association ("NYIPLA") and has been named a "Super Lawyer" for Connecticut and New England every year since it was started in 2006.

Greg is a prolific author, having written more than 55 books on licensing and IP topics, including the seminal book on the law of merchandising entitled *The Law of Merchandise & Character Licensing* which was originally in 1985 published by Thomson Reuters/West and is updated annually. He also writes two annual books for Wolters Kluwer entitled *Licensing Royalty Rates* and *Licensing Update* and is the author of Kluwer's *License Agreements: Forms and Checklists*.

He is a founder and executive editor of *The Licensing Journal* and the *IP Litigator*, both published by Wolters Kluwer, and is the legal columnist for *Total Licensing*, a London based publication. He has written more than 50 articles on various licensing and IP topics and given more qualified as an expert in more than forty actions on licensing related matters.

Greg turned his passion for baseball into a business, having invented a computerized video baseball/softball pitching and cricket bowling simulator which is the subjects of 13 U.S. patents and numerous international patents. He serves as CEO for ProBatter Sports (www.probatter.com) which manufactures and sells ProBatter simulators to a wide range of customers, including a dozen or so Major League teams, scores of college programs, and hundreds of commercial batting cages and training facilities in the United States and 12 other countries.

He can be contacted at gjbattersby@gbiplaw.com.